Opposites and Everything In-Between

Maygen McDougall

authorHOUSE®

AuthorHouse™ UK
1663 Liberty Drive
Bloomington, IN 47403 USA
www.authorhouse.co.uk
Phone: UK TFN: 0800 0148641 (Toll Free inside the UK)
        UK Local: 02036 956322 (+44 20 3695 6322 from outside the UK)

Published by AuthorHouse 09/10/2020

ISBN: 978-1-7283-7920-3 (sc)
ISBN: 978-1-7283-7921-0 (hc)
ISBN: 978-1-7283-7919-7 (e)

Print information available on the last page.

Any people depicted in stock imagery provided by Getty Images are models,
and such images are being used for illustrative purposes only.
Certain stock imagery © Getty Images.

This book is printed on acid-free paper.

For my loved ones, no ones,
and anyone in-between.

The writing you are reading now is made from the cost of living and it is made with digital ink.

—Deborah Levy (*The Cost of Living* 2018, 187)

— 1 —

Sexual Urination in a Cemetery, Tumblr, and Class Struggles

Yesterday I sat in a cemetery, on my own, on a bench. No, I wasn't 'visiting', as they call it, but I was deep in thought. I ended up at the cemetery because I didn't want to arrive too early at my friend Milly's house. Her 21st birthday happened the week before, and I was dropping off her gifts, and she just so happens to live next to a cemetery. I thought it would kill some time to walk through the grounds, sit on a bench, and roll a cigarette.

I sat on the bench and thought about how it is a weird feeling doing something spontaneously, by choice, something totally meaningless. Like when you have a day off and walk aimlessly around the shops. You don't *need* anything; you don't *have* to go—but you do anyway because—because why not? What else are you going to do? I sat on that bench in the spring breeze and felt like I was floating (of course not physically) in existence, with no real purpose or path during these brief moments. Basically, I wondered if it was weird to sit on your own in a graveyard for no real reason …

I rolled my cigarette and considered whether it was disrespectful to smoke in front of the graves. I put together an argument in my head in case someone else at the cemetery decided to tell me off. I mean, yes, 'smoking kills', so to do anything even remotely death-related in front of those less fortunate is a little rude, I guess. But then again, 'they' aren't really there anymore, are they? I don't mind what you believe of course, but I feel like when we die, we just sort of … go. (Unless your spirit turns into a ghost, which are very real, and haunts houses.) I saw people casually walking their dogs along the paths of the cemetery and thought if the dogs peed, they'd have to pee (or *you know*) on the graves. Even the most disciplined of dogs couldn't know where it would be safe to pee. Grass is grass to them. The whole act of urinating on things that aren't toilet related is considered rude—unless you're *into* that. I don't want to fetish-shame but perhaps try and avoid undertaking sexual urination in a graveyard because that would be considered a little controversial to the dead *and* living. So anyway, surely if man's best friend can hypothetically pee on said graves, it would be okay for me to smoke in their presence. I lit my cigarette.

The display laid out in front of me looked like a mismatched scrapbook comprised of old and new, with modern and traditional headstones in uneven rows. Some were eroded by the elements; others were black crystal marble with gold engravings. There was one, a white marble, surrounded by a white picket fence (about three inches in height, a big design flaw for an actual fence). Across the fence were pink ribbons and brand-new toys secured to the sides, clearly a child's grave. Consider me insensitive, but I thought about how much extra attention the child's headstone had received compared to the adults' that surrounded it.

I don't remember the exact names or dates of these adults who are no longer with us, but next to the child's headstone was a rather large concrete one displaying the name of some guy who was in his late 50s at the time of his death. I thought about this man possibly being a husband, brother, uncle, father, friend? He might have broken hearts in his 20s, led by example in his 30s, lived well in his 40s, and died happily in his 50s. (Then again, perhaps he didn't.) He probably met thousands of people in his lifetime, maybe saved a cat from a tree for a child or could've fought in a war. Yet here was his headstone—no attention, no care—left to erode in this Portsmouth graveyard, being stared at by a not-so-physically-floating adolescent.

I see the other side of my own argument though, for why the child's grave receives more acts of love. The child didn't get a chance to break hearts, live well, or save cats; they were not allowed to live life long enough to *live* it. I guess what I'm trying to point out is that these headstones were a morbid metaphor for how society views the older generation. The fact that your life becomes less valuable with the more time and energy you put into it is eye-wateringly depressing and makes me think, *What's the fucking point in anything?* It also illuminates how some innocent children have their lives taken away almost as quickly as they were given them. This too makes me wonder what the fucking point is. We die old, we die young—but for some reason, one outcome is sadder than the other.

See? I told you I was in deep thought. Maybe this is why one shouldn't visit a graveyard for no real reason.

I was suicidal once. That's a weird sentence to

write. I wonder, does someone 'beat' me if they've been suicidal twice? And if someone tells me this, do I have to throw my hands up and say, "Aaaah! You got me; you clearly know sadness better than I do. You win!" I hope not. It doesn't really seem like winning to me. (Although it does say how something about how strong they are, technically overcoming the temptation of death more than once.) Something tells me there are definitely people in the world that believe the fetishized idea of depression.

If you're a similar age to me (I was born in 1999), you'll be very familiar with the Tumblr era of our youths, with young boys and girls posting GIFs of teenagers smoking weed with captions such as "death is only the beginning" and the likes. Users would also post images of their own self-harm scars and captioning their feed as "trigger warnings" as a means to prevent from setting others off into a self-destructive frenzy. Tumblr was a dark time for us all, I feel. If you relate to any of the people who used to participate in this type of behaviour, I really hope you're doing a lot better now. I really do. I understand you just wanted to be seen, *heard*. If you have no idea what a Tumblr account is and don't understand what I've just said, don't worry—that bit wasn't for you. You should be grateful you didn't have to see some of the things I did.

Anyway, I've wanted to die before. It occurred between the ages of 13 and 15, which is scary thinking about it all now—at my wise old age of 21 years and 4 months. Technically, going by my previous research in a cemetery nervously smoking a cigarette, my life was more valuable back then than it is now. Ouch. I won't bore you with many details, mostly because it's all just a clouded haze now, but what I do remember is the constant flux between feeling *everything* and *total numbness*. One of my most vivid memories of my depression was one morning before school. I lay in my bed, surrounded by stereotypical 13 to 15 year-old-girls room décor (feminine wallpaper, cloth tapestry hung from the wall, lots of fairy lights), curtains drawn, little sunlight; and I *couldn't move*. My alarm for school screamed at 7.30am. I turned it off. I rolled onto my side, so my body faced the wall. Tears formed in my eyes. My muscles hurt. My brain hurt. At the same time, I couldn't feel anything. At that moment, I just wanted to die.

Disclaimer: If you feel like this, you're completely justified to speak out or receive profession help. You wouldn't ignore a painful rash, so don't ignore this. I got better, even when I thought I would never be happy again, and so can *you*. It's not easy, but important things never are—if they were, I don't think they'd be important anymore. That doesn't just go for mental health. I think all things are worth fighting for.

I reflect on this moment from time to time and think about how powerful (and slightly sinister) the human mind can be. Nothing was *wrong* with me; my body was in perfect working condition. Yet I remember being thin, weak, grey-skinned, panda-eyed, dull-haired, and spotty. Not saying I'm a prize now, but that was a different type of unattractiveness. It was the worst kind. Someone (me, for example) can be unattractive by popular standards but still look *healthy*. Back then, my mental state had affected me so badly it was visible on the outside. I looked ill, because I was ill. It is this moment back in school (along with *actual* medical science) which leads me to confidently say that mental illness (of all kinds, not exclusively depression) is an actual ailment and not the result of an 'oversensitive generation' as baby boomers love to tell us.

Baby boomers, commonly referred to as just 'boomers', are a generation born between 1944 and 1964. (These dates can vary slightly.) The general consensus of younger generations is that they are undereducated in the liberal ideas surrounding sexuality, race, and gender issues; along with important cultural topics such as technology, politics, religion, crime (do you see a pattern here?), and memes. I mean really, they suck at sharing good memes. (Fun fact: I believe I've just missed the mark on being a millennial myself, being a generation-Z baby born between the years 1995 and 2015—then again, I think these dates are also somewhat flexible.)

You know the type of man that likes to read

The Sun newspaper, drink on their own in Weatherspoons on a Wednesday, and have at least two different people's names tattooed on their arms in script-like-writing. "Oh, Dave, oi, mate, yeah we didn't have depression back in *my day*. Nah, you manned up and got the fuck on with it. That's what *real* men do".

Man, fuck those guys. What's even more confusing is that these are the same types of people that will play the 'men have the highest rate of suicide' card when it comes to issues of feminism. These are the same people that cannot understand similar societal factors like what LGBTQ+ stands for:

> The first four letters of this standard abbreviation are fairly straightforward: 'Lesbian, gay, bisexual, and transgender'. The Q can stand for 'questioning', as in still exploring one's sexuality, or 'queer', or sometimes both. QUEER: Once considered a demeaning slur for being gay, queer is being reclaimed by some as a self-affirming umbrella term, especially among those who consider other labels restrictive. Some still believe it's a homophobic slur, so it's always best to

ask or wait for the person whom you're speaking with to use it. (Emanuella Grinberg, CNN Health Edition, online source, 14 June 2019) https://edition. cnn.com/interactive/2019/06/health/ lgbtq-explainer/

Or how someone can identify as non-binary:

In general terms, 'sex' refers to the biological differences between males and females, such as the genitalia and genetic differences. 'Gender' is more difficult to define, but it can refer to the role of a male or female in society, known as a gender role, or an individual's concept of themselves, or gender identity. Sometimes, a person's genetically assigned sex does not line up with their gender identity. These individuals might refer to themselves as transgender, non-binary, or gender-nonconforming. (Tim Newman Medical News Today, online source, 7 February 2018) https://www.medicalnewstoday. com/articles/232363

It's also people like the 'Karens'—women that yell at sales assistants in shops because they've run out of the special bread they like and say phrases such as, "Oh, Jane, you should've seen her, walking around in nothing but *short*-shorts. No daughter of mine would dress like that". Funny though, because these are the same women who throw themselves at newly turned 18-year-olds in nightclubs and almost always get drunk enough to nip-slip. I understand nip-slips are usually wardrobe malfunctions; I'm just mad at the double standard.

I am aware this is a very stereotypical and quite offensive description that *could* be applied to a majority of working-class British people of a certain age. Please do not think I am writing to you as some silver-spooned-middle-class-white women who thinks she knows better because Daddy said so. I grew up with these types of people; in fact, I can attach these descriptions to a lot of my own family—at least a *few* of the aspects mentioned, anyway. This is a rough estimate, but I believe my own dad has three women's names tattooed on his arm. One is in English and two in Thai. *Don't ask.*

All I'm saying is don't get your knickers in a twist; I adore working-class people. I am one. I was born and raised in a council flat (definition of a CHAV: Council House and Violent) by a single parent, surrounded by tracksuits, Reebok trainers, and Viki Pollards (if you don't know who that is Google it. She is a cultural icon). Some astounding things people of the upper classes never *see* about the working class is their constant resilience, undying work ethic, and ability to tackle the hardest of lifestyles. We grow up in low-income households, surrounded by violence, drugs, and other bad influences. We support ourselves and our dependents with minimum-wage jobs of which we're normally used and abused until fingers bleed because employers are fully aware we have nothing else. We are not told to find our dream jobs or take leaps of faith; we're told to work to purely survive.

I will always have way more respect for people like my dad, who was kicked out of his home at 14, started working on construction sites at 15, continues to work twelve-hour days six days a week and never complains than a guy in a suit who had nannies and support throughout his entire life until adulthood and now works a nine-to-five in an office with a personal assistant to fetch his low-fat, two-pump, almond-syrup coffee every morning. These same types of guys will then talk about how the working class are 'taking up too much housing', not using their privilege to help instead, ignorant to the fact it was people like my dad who *built* the fucking houses. When my mum and I would plan for holidays, or needed to pay an expensive bill, she'd say to me, "Right, Mayg, it's that time again—beans on toast for dinner until it's paid for". I, knowing no different, would reply, "Yes, Mum", and eat beans on toast most days for dinner until Mum could afford to do a substantial food shop.

One memory my mum always brings up in conversations is the time we were in an Iceland food store and I picked something up, showed her, and asked, "Mummy, can we afford this?" Mum shook her head no. So I simply put it back and walked away. According to Mum, I was around 6 years old when I did that. It's interesting looking back now, understanding money and the cost of living better. We really didn't have a lot, but we were so happy.

It is my belief that the working and middle-to-upper classes have their own stereotypes, problems, and idiosyncrasies; I think we can all agree on that. But with this in mind, I will always stand by the fact that if I had to hire someone to work for me, I would always prefer someone from a working-class background to an upper-class one. I feel from experience they'd know what hard work looks like; plus they'd be grateful and eager for the opportunity rather than feel entitled. Also, they add potential to see some nip-slips at work Christmas parties.

I guess my whole point here is that I definitely look a lot better now than I did when I was thirteen or fifteen years old. A little less tired.

2

Schrodinger's Cigarettes and Where to Find Them

Today is a sad day. I ran out of menthol filters. For those of you non-smokers that have no idea what I'm talking about (to which I applaud your clear discipline in social pressure), when you smoke, you can choose between normal 'smoke'-tasting cigarettes or mint-tasting ones. These mint ones are called menthols, and they're the superior type of cigarettes. Unless you have the opinion of my best friend, Georgia, to which she believes that people who smoke menthols are—and I quote—"Pussies".

As of two days ago, the distribution and purchase of all menthol tobacco products became illegal in England. (Well, that's what I thought, until I found them in a Tesco Express one month later.) This was done in an effort to get more people to quit. I guess the people that made this decision share similar opinions to Georgia and believe that if you're a 'real' smoker, you'll only smoke the normal ones. This is ultimately a test to separate the people who see smoking as a fun, tasty habit versus the real committed participants. Survival of the most cancerous, if you will. Irradiating menthols has not made me want to quit or even cut down on smoking. It has simply made the whole habit less *enjoyable*. I still look equally as *cool* as before. I will quit one day, maybe. I hope to quit when I start a professional career, or if I ever become pregnant. I vow to never be someone who smokes during pregnancy. Fair enough if I do this to myself, but another? At least let the kid develop his or her own smoking habit later in life at underage parties like I did. Seems a little unjust giving babies cigarettes at zero months old. Especially non-menthol. Jesus, I'm not a monster.

My first experience with smoking was when I was around 14, and it was all Georgia's fault. Smoking became our 'thing', and we were the kids that waited outside of back-street off licenses and asked, "Oi, mate, 'scuse me, but can you go into the shop for me?"

Not my proudest moment, I'll admit, but I'll also admit it almost always worked.

What made me laugh is that sometimes people would ask, "What for? Fags or alcohol?"

More often than not, when they asked this question and found it was cigarettes we were after rather than booze, they'd say no. This makes me laugh in a cynical way, because that means they'd rather see minors drink than smoke cigarettes. Yes, as I mentioned before I am fully aware smoking kills, but I can't render myself unconscious in a park unsupervised and potentially get molested from smoking too many cigarettes. *Can I?* I do understand these somewhat caring strangers merely didn't want us to get addicted, or at least participate in our addiction to nicotine, but I still don't see their logic even now. I often wonder if asked, *Would I go into the shop for minors?* I mean, on one hand I've been there; I understand what they're going through. On the other, I don't want to risk getting caught and facing legal repercussions. Oh, and do a morally bad thing, I guess.

Now that I'm thinking about it, I think I would. This is because I remember how many no's I received before I got a yes. If I said no, someone else will just say yes. *Eventually.* If these minors are going to be out on the streets talking to strangers, I rather it be me. I would never hurt them, or take advantage of them, or steal their money (happened to me once: a guy bought the packet of cigarettes with our money, got into his car, and drove off. Kept our change as well, the prick). I would love to be able to say I'd talk to them and try to convince them that smoking is a bad habit that makes you smell and ruins your health—but people did that with me back in the day and I am ashamed to admit it just went in one ear and out the other.

Georgia and I now live together, and we are by all sense of the meaning the bestest of friends. I hope you know what I mean by this. Everyone should have a friendship like mine and Georgia's. Don't get me wrong, she is without a doubt the most annoying person I have ever met, and sometimes I daydream about her moving out and how peaceful my life would be if I just saw her for a casual drink sometimes after work. Our friendship relies heavily on some of the most important values that I think should make a friendship of the best-friend kind. These are trust, honesty, reliance, values, and humour. (Do not get trust and reliance mixed up. I mean different things when I list them, although I am fully aware they are by dictionary definition very similar.)

I trust Georgia. I trust her with secrets, juicy

gossip, my life. If a car was about to hit me, I know she'd do her best to save me, even if it meant her own injury or demise. Don't get me wrong. If she pushed me out the way and survived, I'd never hear the end of it. Her ego's big enough; she doesn't need any more encouragement. Part of me would wish I'd been hit.

When I say reliance, I mean I can rely on her to do shit without my even asking her. For example, say I start a fight in a club one night (I'm four feet eleven and weigh approximately forty-nine kilograms, so starting a fight would be silly on my part), I know she'd be there with me fighting. Say something happens and I'm not there to make a decision or say my piece—I know she's got my back and I can rely on her to do my bidding for me.

You're probably thinking *bullshit*, right? But don't be fooled. This level of friendship has taken nine years to develop and has been one of the most challenging aspects of my entire life. *Honestly*. But the best bit about this dynamic we share is that I know everything I say about her she would say about me. I know it sounds incredibly self-centred, but let's just say we've both been in situations where we have proven these aspects and allowed our actions to speak louder than our words. This is key.

My friendship with Georgia has taught me one important thing, and I hope you can learn this too: *It's easy to be someone's friend.* Catch up over coffee, talk about how your boss is a dick, how your student flat is unbearable to live in. Easy. What you need to look out for is the people that stick around when shit gets hard. I'm not talking about the bad day you had because it rained and you missed the bus, I'm talking about the person that holds a meeting with your family behind your back to tell them they don't know what to do to help you on their own anymore, tries to organise professional medical help for you, leaves her house and dumps plans at a moment's notice because one of your texts didn't *read right*. Look for the person that does shit for you, not because it suits them, but because you need it. I've done this for Georgia, and if it meant she'd be okay in the end, I made my peace with the idea she may never speak to me again due to my 'betrayal'. I was willing to lose her to get her back. Better to miss out on future birthday parties than attend a funeral.

It's *easy* to be someone's 'friend'. It's just as easy to walk away when shit gets *hard* (don't make that sexual, I was trying to be serious).

And this is why you may have lots of friends, but only one, or a few, bona fide best friends. If you're reading this and thinking, *I don't have a Georgia*, that's okay. You've obviously made it this far without relying on someone else, without truly trusting anyone in that way, and that makes you strong. Well done. It also means you're not forcing any friendships, which is good too. Take the advice from a girl who would buy cigarettes for minors: if you don't want people around, don't keep them around. I promise you; it might look like your friendship numbers are a little light, but the weight of fake/toxic/forced friends will drown you. So float.

As I sit here writing on my laptop, at my desk, in my two-bedroom flat in Stamshaw, I am smoking a non-menthol roll-up. It's gross. My cat, Luna, is asleep in the middle of my bed, and fairy lights dimly illuminate the room because that's just the type of stereotypical Starbucks-drinking white girl I am. Its currently 3.21am and *Its Always Sunny in Philadelphia* is playing on my TV. I have two framed prints on my desk sitting symmetrically on either side of my laptop. Both were a gift from Georgia for my 21st birthday back in January. She brought them back from her visit to New York. I really loved these prints because I genuinely *liked* them, which made me feel like Georgia knew me very well and that just made the whole gift better. Personal gifts always feel nicer to receive than the obligatory toiletries and gift cards.

One print is an illustration of Snow White eating an apple on a fake cover of *Vogue*. The other is a black and white photograph with red accents. You might know the image; It's called War's End Kiss and it was taken in New York City in 1945. It's a very powerful photograph. It's an image I've seen regularly in shops and printed on mugs and so on. One day during a shopping trip about a year or so ago, my friend Bonnie and I were out and she spotted this photograph in a frame hanging inside a shop. She told me how the photo has been misinterpreted over history and is actually an immortalisation of sexual assault. Allegedly, the women in the photograph doesn't want to be kissed.

When I first saw the prints and saw this photograph was one of them, I didn't mind. In a strange way I kind of liked the fact I know this morbid backstory. It acts as a reminder. When I look at it, I feel like even during a time of liberation, someone as respectable as a soldier can still sexually assault someone. It acts as a reminder that no one seems to really care, since it has become such a famous image. To me, it's powerful in many ways. I'm sorry if you've ever been sexually assaulted, not just women but anyone. And I'm sorry if no one believed you or you've felt like you never had a right to speak out. I don't have a lot of advice for this subject, but I want to tell you I believe you and I see you. It's not fucking fair and you didn't deserve it. I know these words might come across as empty and powerless, but sometimes I think one of the most powerful things we can do in times of injustice is hear one another. Really listen. Sometimes others understanding and valuing your pain as *real* can make a world of difference. It will never undo what's been done, but it could help heal the aftereffects. This is what I can do for you, and I really hope it helps.

If you haven't ever been sexually assaulted or otherwise, I'm happy for you and want you to know you shouldn't feel guilty for that. It isn't a rite of passage despite how common it is. Just be aware, people don't 'avoid' getting sexually assaulted because they were smarter with their decisions or wiser with who they associated with; they don't get assaulted because no one around them was a sexual offender/rapist. It's the offenders' fault, not the victims'. It happens because people rape, not because people allow themselves to be raped.

As I sit here and write, I am overcome with self-awareness. Why am I even writing? Why would anyone value what I have to say? As author Elizabeth Moore said in an interview with *GQ* in 2018, "Writing is unlike almost anything else you will decide to do. It's an undertaking of arrogance, to sit down at a blank page and decide that your opinions, your stories and your experiences are worth turning into words on a page and that others are going to want to read them".

I feel that. I am met with a Schrodinger's cat-type of situation: This book is both being read by someone who went into a bookstore and bought it, aka *you*, or being read by *me*, its author. I am, therefore, struck with the choices to stop writing and give up, eventually dying voiceless, or carry on with uncertainty. I would be lying if I said I didn't like the idea of being heard. It's not that I think I am the smartest or wisest person on earth and everyone *needs* to listen to me; I just think it would be nice to know someone's listening. *Anyone.* I guess I just want to be heard too.

3

I'm a Rude, very Impatient Little Girl

It's May right now. The weather has been highly commendable the past few months; British spring really outdid herself this year. Normally this would be great: sun, sex, beer gardens, and my nicest summer dress. I've just finished my bachelor of arts degree and feel the weight of deadlines lift from my petite shoulders, ready to start the rest of my life (despite the fact I have made the decision to apply for a master's degree—I think I hate myself).

However, the year 2020 and some guy that supposedly decided to eat a bat had other ideas. I am writing to you live from inside the COVID-19 pandemic. If you don't know what that means (where have you been? Or maybe you're reading from the future and haven't had this history lesson yet), basically a virus called the coronavirus has spread around the world, shutting down countries and boarders, stopping a lot of things from functioning as normal. *Worst* of all, it's killed a lot of people. The coronavirus covers many forms of respiratory illnesses, with no treatment or vaccine at the present moment. It's a lot worse than other kinds of viruses and can take up to two weeks for someone to show symptoms, hence the spread and paranoia that follows. I am currently on week either eight or nine in isolation (I can't remember exactly). When I started writing this book, I spoke about how I was sat in a cemetery because I arrived at a friend's house early. If that made you think, *I don't get it, why didn't she just go early?* I hope it makes more sense now. I couldn't enter her home because of the quarantine. Couldn't go sit in a coffee shop because none were open. I can't quite put my finger on it, but I'm sure there is something ironic around the fact that the only place I could go and 'kill' time during a global pandemic was a *cemetery.*

To ensure the virus doesn't spread, the country has been told to not visit people they don't live with, go anywhere they don't need to go, and only leave the house once a day for exercise or food. Due to personal reasons related to her family, Georgia has *needed* to break these rules. You'd think this imbalance in power has caused a rift in our friendship, but it hasn't. It's not her fault she has an obligation to go see her family, whilst I have no good reason to see mine other than I miss them. I know that if I was in her shoes and she was in mine, she'd understand, so I must understand and support her. That's what best friends do. To be honest, this is what anyone should do.

I haven't been able to properly see my family or friends for months, which makes me sad. Especially my mum. She works in a supermarket and is counted as a 'key worker', which means she's one of the people making the UK's world go round right now, next to doctors and nurses and the like (postal workers, Amazon delivery personnel, these types of people too). Thing is, I worked in supermarkets before and remember being abused by customers, being called a 'waste of space' or 'underqualified'— they didn't know or care I was studying at the time and just worked there to pay for nights out (even though I didn't deserve the abuse anyway; I was alright at my job). I would walk to work at 5.30 in the morning, stock shelves, lift and move crates weighing more than me; be on my feet all day, and deal with the idiotic general public all the way until 6pm. Working at the supermarket was one of the worst, most difficult jobs I have ever done. Not only was it manual labour of which everyone had to participate—even the older workers—but the verbal abuse from other staff members and customers made things so much worse. Once, I served a women at the checkout, packed her shopping for her, and engaged in idle chitchat; when she went to walk away, she turned back at me and called me a "rude, very impatient little girl". Fucking boomer. Now, because of this unfortunate series of events, no one can thank supermarket workers more. This makes me angry, because they *always* worked hard, always provided people with food and such; but I guess appreciation is still appreciation even if it's overdue. I just hope that once this pandemic is over the appreciation for the 'underqualified' like my mum will stick around, that way *some* good could come out of this tragedy. Otherwise, if people go back to their normal ignorant values—what was the fucking point in all those claps for the NHS at 8pm on Thursdays? (Fun fact: these claps were very useful in helping me figure out what day it was during weeks of isolation.)

For the past two months or so I have been cleaning anything I can find, unpacking and repacking storage, painting, sewing, watching Netflix, and so on. I'm suspended off work this entire time, of course. My last few months at university were all online. Unbelievable. I attended university for three years, and right at the precipice of my degree a worldwide pandemic unleashes itself. I understand it could be worse: I could be dead! But still, that's really not bloody fair.

Just as my uncle and aunt would say, "Life is shit and then you die". I really like that saying of theirs. It's a little dark, yes, but honest. It has an "it is what it is" energy that I admire.

My family has a few sayings they've coined over the years. One of my dad's favourites is, "You have to drive it like you stole it!" when referring to what kind of driver you should be. He normally shouts it when he *just* makes a green light, or breaks the speed limit.

My stepdad, Charles's, most frequently said phrase is, "Get over it", which has a little backstory to it. When I was a young teenager, between 13 and 15, my mum and Charles brought up the fact I had gotten black nail vanish on his lilac sheets in my room (which wasn't really my room, it was just the spare room in his house). As the very tough, devil-may-care young women I was (a bitch ... I was a bitch), I rolled my eyes, huffed loudly, and said "Get over it!" I then proceeded to storm upstairs.

Now Charles uses it as a form of mockery towards me when someone complains about things they can't change. Mum doesn't really have one particular saying. She just comes out with some profound sentence when the moment deems it necessary. She's not academically bright (although she loves history), but she is wise. I remember when I was in infant school (for those who are international, infant's your first school after nursery) I was having my ICT lessons on the computer. My mum didn't know a thing about technology and would get me to recite my lessons to her on our home computer so she'd also know what to do. I vividly remember being no older than 7 and teaching her how to copy and paste. I sometimes did this with maths as well.

Just like me, Mum loves to learn. I believe I am the first in my entire family to go to university, and that makes me very proud. The fact I now have a degree in media studies kind of waters it down a bit. It's not a BSc in microbiology or anything, but I can tell you how your opinion of something has been formed just by looking at it. Which is something? Although I suppose it is the microbiologists who are attempting to find a cure for the COVID-19 pandemic right now, so I think it's only *fair* they be considered far more educated than I am.

So yes, it's May right now, and we're all experiencing gorgeous weather in the entire United Kingdom—but are unable to go out and enjoy it. This isn't the worst of it for me. I suffer with something called barometric headaches. Basically, changes in the weather cause me to have incredibly painful migraines. I believe it has something to do with pressure, humidity, and the electricity in storms. It means I know when a storm is coming, or when the weather will be really hot and humid. It's basically a superpower with no real benefit to myself or others. So not really a superpower at all, I guess. This links back to what I was saying about how powerful the human mind is. I find it fascinating. I feel like I've got a hyperactive antenna in my brain. I would be lying if I said sometimes I didn't look out the window during one of my episodes and try to control lightning. No luck yet. What would my superhero name be? Electrica? Head-hurts-alota? I could use my powers to zap misogynists in white vans, or people who are mean to animals. They're the worst.

4

Sticks and Stones Are Good for Baseball, and Mansplaining Still Offends Me

Yesterday I told Georgia I was writing this book. She demanded she be allowed to read it. I said no. Anyway, after a very one-sided argument, she yelled, "I *am* your best friend, and I *am* reading it. Am I in it? *You best not put this in it.* Were you nice about me? Have you been mean about me? Oh my God you should write a whole book about me!" I allowed her to read the paragraph about her, and that bit only. That seemed to shut her up. For now. (A few days later she asked to read it again. I said no. She stopped asking after that.)

Today she suggested we take a walk down to the Tipner shoreline near our flat. It was a beautiful day, and since we're in the middle of a worldwide pandemic and nationwide lockdown, my schedule was pretty open. We walked until we found a large square piece of concreate, its original purpose unknown, but I would guess it had something to do with boats or the war. We sat there smoking roll-ups and spoke about feminism, which encouraged a rather healthy debate. Basically, as much as Georgia believes men and women (and anyone otherwise) are equals, she wouldn't call herself a feminist. I, on the other hand, do. I even had 'feminist AF' (an abbreviation for 'as fuck') in my Twitter bio, so you know I meant it. She brought up the time I accused our mutual friend, Patrick, of mansplaining, and argued that I didn't really need to. Her main point was that I had no hard evidence he didn't just explain things unnecessarily to everyone, not just women.

I told her my points; she told me hers. In her defence, I see where she was coming from (to an extent). She just didn't like the idea that I was potentially pushing my feminism onto everything, arguing the reasoning behind certain interactions do not always balance along the fault line of gender. My argument was that I had worked with Patrick for a long time and noticed he only really did it to women; hence my evidence to support he was a typical 'mansplainer'.

Her next point was, did it really matter if that *was* what he was doing? So what if he explained stuff unnecessarily? He wasn't harming anyone, and she didn't think he meant any disrespect by it. I then told her that although, yes, I was unharmed physically by his mansplaining and know very well that Patrick cares for me a lot as a friend, the mental damage can be quite significant. Mansplaining makes me believe you think I'm stupid because I'm a woman. You subliminally think that because I'm female, I mustn't know certain things you do— because of course you're a man and therefore all-knowing. Right?

The boldness of a man explaining things (Patrick explained what withdrawal symptoms are to me and my co-worker, for example) before I even have a chance to ask, "What does that mean?" is incredibly condescending. It's belittling. It's fucking annoying because I don't think someone has ever explained something to me that I didn't already know.

An old friend did it to me once, explaining a simple scientific concept, like condensation or something, and I replied, "Yes. I'm aware. I took GCSE science back in school too, y'know?" He thought he was Einstein, when really anyone older than 16 would almost definitely understand what he meant. Although neither of these conversations resulted in physical harm and where somewhat created from 'wanting me to understand', it does beg the question of why men do it to me, and why doesn't any other gender? Therefore, *it is* something created along the fault line of gender. It is misogynistic, even though it's micro in its effects. Some people do not understand that women may hear mansplaining and start to believe they are as stupid as men think. Women may be told certain things and become manipulated in believing only men have the real answers. Why do you think males dominated society for so long? And still do. Not allowing women the vote is one of the more obvious arguments, but mansplaining is also one. The fact it is so 'unnoticeable' or 'harmless' is the reason it has survived so long and outlived other oppressive structures such as women's ability to vote. This is something Georgia does not understand yet, that feminists such as me must call out people like Patrick, otherwise nothing will change. It will forever be unseen. It will forever be there, oppressing women. Women like her, women like me. To mansplain to me doesn't just mean you're explaining things unnecessarily, it's something deeper, more ingrained. It means you're an active believer (no matter how unaware) of the patriarchal system where men are superior to women and women are the weaker beings. I take it personally. Even if the mansplainer didn't mean it that way.

I like debates with Georgia, because even when we don't agree we still hear the other's argument. I believe these are healthy debates, because they do really make you understand your own points better and potentially spot errors. At the very least, we challenged each other to improve. I also believe that as much as Georgia would hate to admit it, my 'overly feminist' opinions and mind-set were rubbing off on her. It's not just opinions of gender; it's other issues such as sexuality and race. I have never been prouder of her than the time she made a fully comprehendible and accurate argument about the existence of white privilege to her aunt over Chinese take-out once. I didn't even need to help her out—she had it down.

For those of you who are ignorant about the social structure that is white privilege, allow me to explain. I will do this by using a metaphor of children in school. Sorry in advance, but I will try my best to make this simple.

A child is bullied in school. This bullied child represents black people. The bully represents racist white people. The mean, tough bully picks on the child throughout years 3, 4, 5, and so on (these are quite young children). Now, the rest of the students at the school who aren't bullying represent other white people. Not necessarily racists—just white. The students feel sorry for the bullied child, but not enough to stand up to the bully. They don't encourage the bullying, they just stand back and get on with their own lives. They ignore it. The bullied child is insecure, has missed classes out of fear for the bully, and hasn't got any friends because of his 'loser' status. Because of this, he hasn't been able to learn as well as everyone else. He misses out on opportunities because his confidence is non-existent and feels like he can't speak up or be noticed.

As the children all get older, the students that ignored everything go to bigger school and then college, self-esteem being low or high depending on what they've individually gone through—but nothing compared to that of the bullied child. The bullied child grows up less educated and mentally abused. He doesn't amount to much, takes drugs to numb his pain, becomes a 'waste of space' amongst society. This is all he's been taught he's worth. Parents of the children will walk past the now-teenage bullied child and whisper between themselves, "God how awful. He was always a little strange, maybe because of his homelife or something. Disgusting". You know the type of conversation, normally exchanged between two blonde, white, middle-class, middle-aged women— one called Karen and the other Jane.

White privilege is something all white people have. With this privilege, you have ignorance to not know what it's like to be treated differently because of the colour of your skin. Not only that, a white person often has the power to potentially stop a bully but doesn't. White privilege *doesn't* mean your *life hasn't been hard.* It means it hasn't been made *harder* because of your race. It doesn't mean you're *automatically* a racist either. Because of how they look, people of colour have a harder time living—anything you've found hard as a white person, they've found even harder as a black person because of racism and oppression. The classes the bullied kid missed out on is a metaphor for lost jobs or scholarships. The fact that he is undereducated is a metaphor for the fact that neighbourhoods with majority black and brown communities are underfunded and often below standards. The fact the two parents couldn't see the reasons the bullied child turns to drugs, crime, and all those other awful things was because he was bullied by the white racist shows the ignorance many white people have. Not only do we cause the oppression black people go through, we chose to ignore that it was us white people that started it.

That section got a bit heavy, didn't it? But if you didn't know what white privilege was, it was a lesson you *needed* to hear. Sorry if you're a person of colour reading this and you feel like that metaphor was rather shitty and didn't really do anything justice—I promise it was coming from a good place, and I tried my best to use my white privilege for the better. Maybe that's what I'll use my lightning control powers for—to zap racists! I hope if you're white and are reading this, you're more aware of your privilege now. More importantly, if you see someone being bullied, don't ignore it. Speak up. It is the voices of angry people that will change history.

Georgia and I finished our visit to the shore with a game of makeshift baseball. We used a medium-sized stick we found (that really had no business being on a beach) as a bat and stones as balls.

Georgia asked, "Do you think people think we're weird?"

With that question, I was thrown into a sense of outer-body awareness. I wonder what *I* would think of two women in their early 20s playing a game of modified baseball with a stick and stones on a beach in the sun. I think I'd be jealous I wasn't involved. I thought it looked like we were having innocent fun, which we were. Then again, we were in Stamshaw, so maybe onlookers where just thinking we were losers and wondered how'd they beat us up.

5

Between a Puffy Dress and a Hard Place

A few weeks ago I bought three new dresses for the upcoming summer months (unaware how long isolations would last). The vibe I was going for was old-English tea party, if you can imagine such a thing. There was one tailored, black and white dress with a string waistband; another was a red and pink floral dress that puffed out slightly as the bottom. The third was a plain green dress that didn't have a lot of tailoring to it. In fact, it looked like a baggy T-shirt with ruffled sleeves.

I tried on all three dresses and sent pictures I had taken in the mirror to my mum. I don't know why I did this, maybe I just needed gratification that I *can* dress feminine from time to time. Like one morning when I met my dad for breakfast and the shop I was working for at the time made me wear one of their dresses for uniform. Dad saw me, stopped in his tracks, and said, "Wow, babe! You look like a *woman* today!"

Thanks, Dad. Worst bit was, I didn't even like the dress that much. My mum loves me an awful lot, probably more than anything; however, she doesn't always like how I dress. My go-to clothes consist of jeans, baggy T-shirts or jumper (depending on the weather), and Doc Marten shoes or boots. If you can imagine, my mum often says "Why do you cover up like that? You have an amazing figure! Why don't you buy clothes that fit you?" and so on.

I just feel most comfortable in baggy clothes. I think the 1970s, '80s, and '90s aesthetic style of clothes are super cool, and I try to imitate vintage looks. I think where my and my mum's opinions differ on style is just a generational thing, because people my own age always compliment my style, which makes me feel a lot better. One really sweet gesture my mum did once was buy me a pair of tailored pink, white, and purple chequered trousers for Christmas just gone. I knew she didn't like them, but when I opened them up, she said, "I saw them and thought they were very *you*".

This was one of the most supportive gestures she has ever made, and I don't think she knew quite how much it meant to me. I really do like those trousers.

My mum viewed my mirror-selfie pictures in the new dresses and told me she loved them! However: "Not too sure" on the green one. This, going by history, wasn't at all surprising.

I replied, "Yeah, it's probably just an around-the-house dress".

Thing is, as I later discovered, it was my favourite out of the three. I've worn it around the house, to the shops, to the beach with Georgia, and even to bed. The fabric was so comfy, and where it had no tailoring, it felt so liberating to wear. You couldn't really see where my bust started, or where my stomach was. It was like a parachute. The dress was a really sweet mint green, and I felt like it went well with my mousy brown hair and hazel eyes.

Yesterday I brought three more of this same dress in yellow, baby pink, and maroon. I'm excited for them to arrive. When I wear this dress, I can't stop thinking about this puffy black dress my dear friend Bonnie wore to a party once, about two years ago. I can't remember exactly what happened, but someone (a heterosexual man) commented on Bonnie's figure, which made her say something that's stuck with me ever since. I vividly remember her shouting over the loud music, "For God's sake, I wore this dress so you couldn't even *see* anything!" This black puffy dress looked very nice on her, but she was right; you couldn't see anything. It was too puffy.

This stuck with me because I realised the sexualisation of certain aspects of the body isn't always a good thing—she had purposely covered something attractive so it wouldn't be seen. My mum wasn't 'too sure' about my green dress because it was the least tailored of the three; however, it is the one I feel most comfortable in. I feel quite content with my body, just as I'm confident Bonnie is with hers, yet we both choose to hide them. I guess we share the idea that if no one can see anything, no attention (flattering or otherwise) can be paid to us, which makes us more comfortable. I do like the idea that if a guy or girl (or another sort of gender identification) tries to 'chat me up' in a bar, they'll do it because of my face, or my vibes, or something romantic like that rather than because my bum looks good. Our bodies are the prize they'd win if they proved themselves worthy enough to receive it.

Georgia has rather large boobs (unlike mine, which are very small—in fact one of the nicknames my friends have for me is Boy Tits), and she has mixed feelings about them. Sometimes she'll try on a dress and say, "It's too booby", or "My boobs look good in this". I think if you've got big boobs and show a lot of cleavage in a low-cut top, for example, that is completely and utterly fine. They're part of your body. When people call women horrible slut-shaming words like 'whore', 'prozzy', or 'desperate' because they're showing their body, it infuriates me. That's like saying the likes of Georgia should be ashamed of their breasts.

I guess what I'm trying to say is: if you see a girl in a revealing dress, just don't say anything. If you see someone is covered up even if it's warm out, don't say anything. You don't know what anxieties they have and where they came from. Maybe if people stop saying unneeded comments, women won't feel the need to be ashamed of their big boobs. Maybe if people keep their mouths shut, the likes of Bonnie won't feel objectified anymore. The double standards make for very little space in which women can feel comfortable. We're caught between a puffy dress and a hard place.

Yes, I am aware these issues of anxiety and body dysmorphia are shared with men (or anyone otherwise) too. The same rules apply. If you see a person afraid to take his or her top off in the pool, let it be. If you see an exceedingly tall person, you probably don't need to point it out—it's likely that he or she is probably aware.

There are concepts around clothing and people revealing their bodies which make my blood boil. Let's just say I don't have a 'let it be' approach to everything. I'm talking about something that happened to me.

One night, friends and I went out drinking, and I got very drunk. I had been friends with these people a long time and we had all been drunk together before. No issue. I was so drunk I spilt not one but two drinks over myself. The second time around, my dress was drenched in beer. A male friend offered me the plaid shirt he was wearing over his T-shirt for me to wear as a dress. I'm very petite, and his shirt was the appropriate size. In the toilets I put my wet dress in my bag and put his shirt on.

I continued the rest of the night wearing his shirt as a dress. When the pub shut, Georgia and I often took the party back to our flat, and that is what we did this night. When I got home, I changed from my friend's shirt to one of my own baggy T-shirts. I either got changed in the privacy of my own bedroom or bathroom—I can't remember that *one* detail—but I was alone. I wore this oversized, baggy T-shirt and pants and nothing else, but I was in my own home surrounded by familiar people, so even drunk I felt like there was no issue with this. By the way, I still don't.

I guess I'm not as comfortable talking about this night as I thought, but I'll just say that the male friend whose shirt I borrowed stayed in my bed that night. I did not invite him; I did not encourage this. He was my *friend,* and even drunk, I vividly remember not seeing him as anything romantic.

The next morning I was angry at Georgia. "Why didn't you stop him? Didn't you hear him come into my room? Surely you knew I wouldn't want that".

It's interesting, looking back, because I've realised I was angrier at her for not stopping it, and myself for 'allowing' it to happen, than I was at my male friend for *doing it.* I think this speaks volumes for how society views occurrences like this. Like we expect them to happen—we predict them. We blame the victims and the ones who 'could've done something' to prevent it from happening, but not so much the guilty parties themselves. It was his fault for what happened, not mine or Georgia's. I know this now, but it doesn't take away from the fact I should've know this straight away—and how others must feel in their own experiences.

I made excuses for him: "He was drunk too", "He misunderstood the situation", "Oh, he must like me like *that;* poor guy doesn't know I don't feel the same about him". Again, with hindsight, I think about myself possibly doing something *like that. Would I* do something like that? *Could I* possibly do the same mistakes he did, rendering the whole thing a simple miscommunication blamed on human error? No, I really, *really* don't think I ever would, or have ever, done something similar. I would just feel *wrong*.

So if that's the case, why did he do it?

I felt gross for a while after this night (sometimes I get random flashbacks, but nothing too major), and I didn't want to look at or talk to my male friend for a while. In due course, I confronted him. I said he took advantage, told him I remember *not* inviting him into my room at any point, and so on. I explained I was clearly drunk.

He stood there in my kitchen and listened, silent, nodding sometimes. He apologised for his actions but said, "I feel like you're twisting things a bit. You were in my shirt. You were walking around in nothing but a T-shirt. I thought that was a sign".

When I say that this made me furious, I think even that is an understatement. I was livid. Enraged. How fucking dare someone be so entitled, so ignorant to the rules of consent, the code of friendship! I was in his shirt because I was wet, and then I was wearing what was comfortable in my own home! Even if I decided to walk around naked, *naked is still not consent. naked is not a fucking 'sign'*!

There was another male friend of mine that night, along with Georgia—was it a sign for them too? Like me in a baggy T-shirt and pants is code for a gang bang? Oh no, wait. *I was wearing his shirt for a bit, so of course it was just a sign for him.*

Showing skin is not consent.

Lots of no's and a singular yes is not consent.

Someone being drunk whilst you're sober is not consent.

Giving you a basic compliment is not consent on its own.

Wearing pretty underwear over or under clothing is not consent.

Someone being under the age of consent, whilst you're over the age of consent, despite the fact he or she might be saying yes is still not legally consent.

Rendering themselves unconscious does not mean you don't need to ask for consent and you can do what you want to them.

People's clothing doesn't tell you whether they want to fuck you; if they're in the right frame of mind and willing, they will be able to clearly tell you *themselves*. If they can't, or it's not clear, stay the fuck away. In short: just don't sexually assault or rape anyone. Is that too much to ask? It's currently 2020, and people need to do better. I do not believe *all* men are capable of these wrongdoings. I do not believe it is *just* men who can do these wrongdoings. I've heard stories from three other male friends who said they've been sexually assaulted, two by women and one by a man. This is not a message to anyone specific. Think of it as a lesson for everyone. I do not like the fact that we *teach* people self-defence to prevent rape. I do not like the fact rape whistles exist. I do not like the fact I was *taught* to walk with keys in between my fingers walking home late at night to use as a possible weapon against rapists. Let's stop teaching people how to protect against these sorts of attacks like they're a normalised part of society. Why don't we teach people to not rape instead? Surely fighting this at the *source* is more effective. Maybe if my male friend was educated in these issues, he wouldn't have done what he did. Perhaps if women aren't told, "You might get raped or assaulted if you get too drunk at that party", we'll see it more as an issue enough to speak out—rather than just accepting it was probably our fault for drinking too much.

Also, whilst I'm here: What the fuck is the deal with people not normalising periods? Seriously? I remember so clearly being in school around 8 or 9 years old during our *two-day-long* sex-ed lesson.

(I don't think two days is long enough, and I think we were taught it too late.) Boys were separated into one room, girls into another. *Why?* Why can't men learn about periods? People with periods have been ingrained to hide them. Why? They're seen as mysterious and gross, which is incredibly condescending at the very least. Why are penises seen as too rude for women to see or discuss in class? Surely we should know how they work too.

I'm sorry if this bit isn't very gender neutral; please note I do see you nonbinaries and anyone else who doesn't identify as a man or women. I'm *still* continuing to educate myself enough in order to embed you into this description and others. I know you're out there with your own set of just as valuable concerns and the issues that follow them. I am taking my own advice and losing my ignorance. I don't know everything just yet, and *I can still do better.*

This actually includes you guys too, because if everyone was in the same room learning sexual education about everyone (not just their assigned genders or biological sex), it might have helped you understand yourselves better, or at least gave you the option to assess all information and interpreted it as you wanted it to, rather than being *told* what you are and how you worked. I'm not an educator of any kind academically, and arguments could be made to suggest I am not an educator *at all*, but I do believe it is very harmful to a lot of people to separate the classes during sexual education lessons, and to see just how little is actually taught for an awful lot of reasons. The lack of clarity with a lot of these pretty basic aspects of life like consent, periods, and penises are still so alien to people. Yet almost all of us have sex (shout-out to my virgins, you'll get there, *if you choose to*), and we mostly all have or know people who have periods and penises.

There is technically no excuse to explain where this unfamiliarity came from. Things that have no business being sexualised have been twisted into forbidden topics. It's nature, it's normal, it's fucking reproduction. There is literally a TV show called *One Born Every Minute,* which shows activities taking place in the labour ward, yet no one can speak about *how* one is born every minute. But it's every fucking minute? Normalise this shit. Jesus Christ. This is all in the same category about how women who admit they masturbate are sexual deviants yet men who masturbate are normal and 'just need to release'. What the fuck are you releasing? Your oppression? Toxic masculinity?

Long day of mansplaining? Goddamn. I'd argue I need it more than you do, after being called a very rude, impatient little girl by a boomer after working a twelve-hour-day in a supermarket. But no, I'm apparently a sex addict. Or perhaps me talking about masturbation is considered a 'sign', and then if I'm ever sexually assaulted again, it's also my fault, right?

As I said earlier, its 2020, and we need to do better.

6

I'm Not Sorry

When I was 18, I moved away to Brighton for university with my then boyfriend (who I will call Leech. I do not wish to name him and make him somewhat 'famous'. He earned this nickname towards the end of our break-up and hated it).

Anyway, Leech and I decided to get a cat together to make the perfect addition to our home. At the time I was very happy. We had a tiny, overpriced flat in Kemptown but it was *ours*. I did my absolute best to make the studio-like flat a home for us. We brought Luna, a black Persian-cross, for £150 at 9 weeks old . She was the fluffiest ball of energy with the biggest blue-green eyes. So innocent. Leech and I loved her pretty much instantly, and as much as Leech was an all-time dickhead (as I later discovered), he was a very good owner to her.

The reason I bring this up is because she was the first living thing I had parent-like responsibility for. There are no young children in my family and I am an only child—so as far as children go, I am at a loss. I've never even babysat a cousin's sister's friend's kid one time in summer holidays. Mum and I had cats whilst I was growing up, but when you're a child, you feel like the parents take most (if not all) responsibly, which my mum did.

So there I was, completely overtaken with maternal instincts for this small black kitten. She was my *baby,* and I'm a little ashamed to admit still is. Leech and I had signed a contract to say we wouldn't have pets of any kind in the flat, so when estate agents would come for inspections, we would have to hide all her things (litter box, food bowl, toys, and so on) in the kitchen cupboards whilst one of us took her for a walk in our arms around the block. I remember thinking, *I swear, if they tell me we have to get rid of her, I'm going to move out because she isn't going anywhere.* I got angry, making up scenarios in my head about non-existent conversations with the landlords. This is weird to an extent because I was willing to lose my home I had so lovingly created for a cat. But I also don't think it's weird, because as the famous saying goes, "A dog isn't just for Christmas" (yes I know it says dog but it can mean cats as well). I couldn't rehome her—how would the new owners treat her? What would they feed her? No! Nope! I would seriously murder for that little ball of fluff that is currently shitting in her litterbox by my front door. Yes. She is staying with me and that is final (which is why I got custody of her after the break-up).

Luckily for us, we never got caught harbouring a cat.

If what I feel towards Luna is a drop in the ocean compared to what my mum feels for me (which I do believe is the case; I am aware cats and children are very different), then I have decided being a parent to a human being is the most bittersweet thing in the entire world: Bitter in its fear, anger, and protection, and sweet in its fulfilment, fun, and love. I guess this is something I can potentially look forward to. I say potentially because I don't like the fact women are *expected* to have children.

Like when I was young, I was told, "When you grow up and have babies of your own …" I've realised no one ever said, "When you grow up and decide if you want babies of your own …" It dawned on me that I completely forgot I have a *choice*. Did you realise that? You can literally say no to having kids? This new realisation is incredibly empowering, and it makes me feel a lot better. If I have a child, it will because I wanted to, not because that's what being a women is about. Because it's not. Being a women doesn't mean you must breed—although it is an additional thing people with female sex organs and reproductive systems can do. Trans women are women too. Asexual women are women too. If you're a women, you're a women, and that's that. (Or at least, that should be the way it is.)

When Luna was 6 months old, Leech and I decided to get her spayed, which means she is unable to have urges to mate and have a litter of her own. We thought this was best because she is a housecat and didn't want to risk her running off when she felt like it. We also didn't want her having babies because we didn't like the idea of having more kittens and having to sell them. I know that if she did, I'd love them all too much to sell them.

We picked her up from the vet's and took her home, and she was high as shit. It was adorable and really funny to watch her walk backwards around the living room for no reason. When I went to bed that night, she jumped up on my pillow and placed herself next to my head. When I say next to, I mean I was breathing in fluff because of her close proximity. She then placed her own head on my forehead and fell asleep. She slept there all night.

And the night after. Luna isn't a very affectionate cat normally; she nudges me for attention every so often but otherwise is quite happy at a distance. The nights she slept on my face, at a time she must have felt achy and vulnerable because of her surgery; I *knew*. I knew she knew I was there to keep her safe. It was proof she didn't just see me as a food dispenser but as her guardian. I was happy sleeping completely still for those nights, inhaling hairs with every breath. I was happy to be her comfort—I felt like I was a good 'parent' and that made me all fuzzy inside. But maybe that's because my lungs where filling up with Persian-cross DNA.

I do wonder what type of parent I'd be. I know I can't say for certain until I actually have a child of my own, but I like to guess. I hope I'm fair, understanding, a 'cool' mum. I want to be like my mum. I wouldn't mind being a little like my dad either. I even want to be like my stepdad. He came into my life when I was 13, so I was pretty much past the point of 'training' by then. But I certainly learned a lot of things from observing him all these years. He's calm and calculated. He knows a lot about a lot. He's a great man, my stepdad—and nothing makes me more content than knowing my mum and Charles are incredibly in love. I suppose in a way I have attributes from all three of my parents. I have my dad's violent tendencies; I think that's because we're Scottish. I also have his humour and his adventurous spirit. I have my mum's heart (or at least I hope I do), and I guess I think like her, which I like. I don't know exactly what I got from Charles, but sometimes I find myself in situations and think, "What would Charles do?" and it tends to help. So I thank him for that.

I have this idea that we're all working titles of our own personalities, and the people we love, hate, know, or knew all add to it. I'm terrified of commitment to men now because of Leech, I blame Georgia for my music taste (and nicotine addiction), and I found out I had somewhat maternal instincts from Luna. If I sat down and pinpointed attributes, values, and traits I have gained from others, I could probably explain every single piece of my personality. You probably could too. Which is why whenever asked the questions, "Do you have any regrets?" or "If you could, would you change anything in your past?" I always say no. Yes I've felt pain, betrayal, a life without nicotine … but I wouldn't be who I am now if those things changed. So thank you to Leech and others who hurt me, because I've learned to deal with pain, heartbreak, and stress. Thank you to friends I've fallen out with, you made me realise how poisonous gossip is. Thank you to the Prick Who Stole My Cigarettes, because I learned to get the packet *off* people *before* they got in their cars from then on. We live, we hurt, we heal, and we grow. I'm only 21 and 4 months and am painfully aware I haven't even felt *half* of it yet. I still could be a parent; I still have to suffer grief of losing a loved one. As my uncle and aunt say, "Life is shit and then you die", and I don't think they could be any more correct. I'm okay with that. I guess *I'll just drive it like I stole it, and get over it.*

My and Leech's relationship came to an end

after two and a half years. This was because I couldn't see how toxic it really was for a very long time. Realistically, it probably should've ended after about a year. Sometimes I'll be sat on the bus or washing the dishes and remember conversations we had; how vile he used to be. I get angry and think, *Why did I just sit there and take it?* He was never physically abusive (I'm not thanking him for that, just making sure I'm not implying anything false). In fact, I was physical once: I threw a Doc Marten boot at his head with all my might. He got very condescending when it hit him and he said, "Well, that was unnecessary, wasn't it?" I can't remember if I threw it jokingly or not.

One of the most painful moments of our relationship was one night in our Brighton flat, around 2am. I had a feeling he was up to something. I had felt this feeling before, so I went on his phone whilst he slept. No, this isn't good, I confess. It didn't help either because I found evidence to suggest he was speaking with other women over Instagram. I immediately woke him up, and we addressed what happened. I apologised for going through his phone, and he assured me I had nothing to worry about. The second time the same thing happened, I woke him up, I addressed what I had found (the evidence had doubled since the first time), but this time he just looked *straight at me*, stone cold in the face and said, "I'm not sorry".

Those words still ring sharp even now. I just couldn't understand it. I loved him so much. I made our house a home. I was loyal. I listened to him. Gave him attention. Gave him space. I made myself pretty for him even when we weren't going anywhere special. I tried to make him laugh as often as I could. I opened myself up to him, in all sense of the words. I saw nothing but him. Yet here he was, looking at the woman who had sacrificed so much, put him before herself, in pain, shaking out of jealously and betrayal … and all he had to say was, "I'm not sorry".

The admittance of wrongdoing, the brute honesty of guilt-free actions. Wow. *What a fucking psychopath.* And how fucking crazy in love was I? I stayed with this cunt for another year or so after that awful night. His presence still haunts me even now in his absence. The thought of someone having that much control over my emotions, my being *dry heaves* so vulnerable. Nope. Nope. I am single and thriving, and until I meet someone good enough (if that day ever comes, I don't mind if it doesn't) I will stay this way. I've never felt better than being single. No one to answer to, no one to cheat on me or make me feel small (metaphorically, I will always feel small physically, but I am at peace with that). Me and my cat against the world. I'm starting to think crazy cat ladies are cultural icons like Vicky Pollard. (For my international readers, Vicky is an obnoxious teenager on the show *Little Britain*.)

This is why he's being addressed as Leech—he does not deserve to be named. Is that petty of me? I suppose what I learned from this relationship is self-worth. Weird how I learned self-worth whilst spending time with someone who didn't appreciate me. I think what made me learn this valuable lesson was watching him, *seeing him* for the first time without the rose-tinted glasses. He was lazy, rude, arrogant, a classic middle child, selfish, ungrateful, and not that great in bed. Yet here I was, hopefully the opposite of those things. Cheat on *me,* will you? Fine, girls you can fucking have him—I insist. Take him off my hands. I'm done.

I went from, "No, don't leave me; I love you!" to "I'm leaving you; I don't love you!" And honestly, it's an amazing feeling. After our break-up we still catch up from time to time. Despite my dislike for the guy, our natural chemistry is undeniable.

He stopped by my flat only recently, as he bought

a kitten for his new flat and I said I'd give him some of Luna's old things for the new kitten to use. He came by with his new girlfriend, Kimberly. He stood there and asked, "How's your dad? Dead yet?"

I said no, and then looked straight at Kimberly (who was silent the entire time). Is it things like that I used to look past? Honestly, I just felt sorry for her the entire time. Kimberly left with Luna's things and took them to the car, which gave Leech and me time to talk alone.

"Here, Mayg, you know I'm great in bed, right?" he asked, keeping his voice low as to not be heard. I regret never telling him he never satisfied.

"Hmmm", I replied.

"Well, the other day, I was fuckin' 'er, and afterwards we realised I'd made her bleed!" he told me, laughing.

"What on earth?" I was thrown off guard by this information. Did he used to speak about me like that? "Sounds like you must have ripped or torn something *down there*", I calmly suggested. It's not like it was her fault or should be embarrassing to her.

"Yeah, she said that has never happened before. I think I just fucked her too hard!" He was smiling the entire time.

I can't believe (well, actually, I can) he thought that was evidence of a good, appropriate sexual performance. In our entire time together, he never made me orgasm, not even close—yet marks on my body or injury through rough sex was always his bragging point. Wow. I was so blind; perhaps so is she? I'm once again not suggesting Leech was ever physically abusive, nor am I saying he intended to make Kimberly bleed—but wow. His reaction speaks volumes for how he, and perhaps other heterosexual cisgender males, view sex. The fact an injury that was not common practice to her (or linked to periods) that actual resulted in Kimberly bleeding made him proud. Not only that, but he told me? His ex? Was that supposed to make me jealous? Like, "Oh no, what have I done? He never made me bleed through aggressive sex before, lucky bitch".

It's kind of funny when you think about it. Kimberly, if you're reading this, I'm sorry I told people he made you bleed during sex. Also, leave him. Run. He won't make you cum, and he'll probably get you to pay for everything.

7

I Really Fancy Actor Tom Holland

Today I realised I think a lot. Like, *constantly*. I don't know if everyone is like this, but I hope it's not just me. In the bath washing my hair yesterday, I thought about the stigmatisation around tattoos. Today whilst doing chores, smoking cigarettes and cooking cup-of-soups, I also thought about the reasons men hate feminism so much, actor Tom Holland (I just *really* fancy him), pro-life debates, racist police in America, and gun-control laws. Did you know it's easier for a minor to buy a gun in some states than alcohol?

I realised my brain never turns off. When Georgia and I were sat on the beach talking about our friend Patrick being a mansplainer (our opinions on this still in disagreement), I said to her, "Sometimes I wish I could just forget it all. I really wish I was ignorant, naïve to all these issues", and I meant it.

I wish I could think about nothing, just sometimes. I want a break. I have come to the realisation I think all the time and am starting to wonder if it's bad for me. The things I think about are always heavy, always serious, and often completely out of my hands. I like to believe that just like any other feminist aware of her white privilege and who's pro-abortion, if I keep voicing my opinions, soon, *something* will be heard. I mean, that's why we do it, isn't it? To be heard, so things can change—hopefully for the benefit of everyone. However, I'm now starting to think that maybe this is why I'm stressed all the time. Maybe this is why I am in constant breakouts. Maybe this is why I am unable to sleep at night. It's true that I'm a very spotty, tired, and stressed-out person—I never really knew why; I just assumed that was part of being 21.

I don't think I help myself with all these thoughts, though I never really speak about them. Yes, Georgia and I will have the odd debate but not often enough to be considered a suitable about for me to vent. As I said, I think a *lot* of stuff. I do have these amazing conversations with my friend Bonnie, the friend who wore the puffy black dress to that party. When we get together, it's like fireworks! Bouncing and exploding intellectual conversations and a lot of "Oh did you see this in the news recently?" or "Have you see this video?" or "Did you hear about this woman who …" I don't see Bonnie very often, though.

I asked her to send me a list of book recommendations yesterday. I'm not a big reader but I'm trying to be. I finished Deborah Levy's *The Cost of Living* (2018) just last week and feel inspired. I think that's what made me start writing this book. Bonnie rose to the request as I knew she would and today in the post arrived *New Erotica for Feminists: Satirical Fantasies of Love, Lust, and Equal Pay* (various authors, 2018), *Why I'm no Longer Talking to White People about Race* (Reni Eddo-Lodge, 2017), and *The Unexpected Joy of Being Single* (Catherine Grey, 2018).

This is what I mean by 'I don't think I help myself'. I know by reading these I'm going to be more read-up on certain social and cultural issues—therefore probably *more* stressed out and angry about them than before. I don't like talking about feminism, racism, and other political/social/ economic issues a lot because I don't want to be labelled 'that girl'. I don't want to open my mouth and be met with eye rolls from people I thought were supposed to listen. I adore my friends. I really do. I'm very lucky to have the ones I have, but I am already known by the majority as 'the feminist', and I don't think even my female friends really mean it in a good way. Little do they know I don't talk about any of it as much as I want to. Little do they know I have tried to shut up and be less annoying, less preachy—but I just *can't*. I wish they were on the same level of 'woke' as me, so that way I wouldn't feel the need to say anything at all, and when I did, I wouldn't feel like 'that girl'. I also know that shouting things at them and metaphorically stuffing feminism down their throats won't help either; in fact, it would probably make them more misogynistic (again, even the females). So here I am, along with a lot of other people, saving my feminism and #BlackLivesMatter speeches for the only place that listens: Twitter.

Maybe one day Tom Holland will follow me on Twitter. A girl can only dream.

This structure doesn't seem very fair, though. What is it about things like activism that gets people so angry? So annoyed? Activists, for the most part, just want to help. Why aren't all women 'feminists'? Scratch that. Why isn't everyone? Men, women, nonbinary, trans—anyone. Feminism is the social, political, and economic equality of the sexes. Hear that? *Sexes*. Multiple. It doesn't mean women power, it doesn't mean all men must die, it doesn't mean we reverse the oppression put on women. It means it should be okay for a guy to be a stay-at-home-dad whilst his wife is the breadwinner without any stigmatisation towards *either* of them. It means emotional women are stopped being addressed as hysterical whilst emotional men can stop being called 'female' for showing emotion (as if female should ever be considered negative!). How can people not see this? Feminists want the best for men and others, not just women. Saying it louder for the people in the back: equality of the *sexes*.

I think men who get offended by feminism are just flat-out misogynists. They have this warped perception where they think feminists are just crazy and are fighting an unnecessary cause. "Women have equal rights! What more do they want?" they say. "Oh, they don't want equal treatment; they want special treatment because they're women!"

I laugh when I hear these types of sentences. It is so obvious they don't know anything about the activism feminists have actually done; they have no idea what we actually stand for. I have read a lot of content on feminism, academically and on Twitter (which I would actually argue is academic at times). I have studied it for my degree, in my spare time, and I have a large amount of men and women friends, and most importantly, I have been a women for 21+ years. Fellas, guys, nonbinaries, anyone who thinks that feminism is a waste of time, take it from me: I promise you, it's worth every single burning bra. If you don't believe me, just fucking Google it. If you spent more time *researching the cause you hate so much, you might actually stop hating it.*

Imagine the audacity of someone trying to comment on an activism movement they know nothing about and thinking they're completely correct for no fucking reason at all? Hilarious. I think they feel threatened that they won't get the next promotion because their female colleague will get it instead—perhaps he believes the only reason why she got it is because she is a women and the company wanted to seem all-inclusive. Dudes, really?

I watched an Oprah interview a few weeks ago, and she was talking about the time she asked her boss why she and her male co-worker had a giant pay gap despite doing the same job. Her boss replied, "Why do you need to make the same as he makes? You're a women". (I may be paraphrasing, but that's the gist.)

Guys, this was the 1980s. Not the 1600s, not centuries ago—the '80s. People who believed this type of patriarchal structure can still be alive, well, and thriving today. This is the shit we want to stop. We don't want your job; we want our own. We don't want your money; we want our own. We don't want your spotlight; we want to get rid of the spotlight completely so no one is socially more important than the other. If this is what you're afraid of, then not only are you a misogynist, you're the worst kind. You're aware of your privilege and don't like the idea of giving it up. To that I say, with the upmost disrespect, fuck you the hardest.

If you find me annoying and want to stop hearing about it all, not just the feminism but everything (racism, homophobia, transphobia—things like this and more), then help. A. Bitch. Out. You think I want to explain white privilege to white people every day? You think I like explaining to strange men on the bus why telling me to "Smile!" is problematic? Fuck no! I'm bored! I'm tired! I'm fucking stressed! I just wanna take over the planet and scream, "Just fucking listen to me!" whilst crying and shaking. I'm not trying to come across egotistically or like I know better than everyone—because I don't think that at all. Honestly. I just think I know more than *some* people about *certain* things, important things. Like many activists, or anyone really, I just want to be heard.

I got very angry writing that. I'm going to roll a cigarette now.

Okay, I'm back. I smoked in my kitchen, had a solo dance to some Lizzo songs playing from my speaker, and now feel much better. As Lizzo famously says, "I just took a DNA test. Turns out I'm one hundred per cent *that bitch*". Words to live by. Truly inspirational. I want those words on my gravestone.

I guess there is only so-angry I'm allowed to be. I'm embarrassed by this, but I used to *hate* feminists. I remember clearly listening to feminism topics on the television with Leech, and we'd scoff and say, "Pfftt, really?" I never understood them. All I saw where 'social justice warriors' finding errors in daily life and complaining relentlessly about them. I used to see pointless, weak arguments about inequality and laugh at how stupid the women on the tele were. It wasn't just feminists; it was all activists. I didn't *see* what they were all so angry about. This is also why I'm not that angry at some of Georgia's points of view; I was her once.

University was my turning point. I make jokes about how media studies is a 'mickey mouse degree' and such, but I don't mean it at all. I stand by my chosen field. It allowed me to see the world differently and thus learn about all these causes I used to hate. It was only until I was educated in them, like, really researched, that I was able to understand why everyone was so angry. A peaceful veil had been lifted and my ignorance was stripped from me. Don't be discouraged; I understand some hear the word 'university' and think of stuck-up academics and 'know-it-alls'. I can't speak for every degree, but mine wasn't like that. My research was more or less what people can do in university or not.

I read a paper (yes, it was an academic paper, but just wait) on audience participation. It illuminated how when female media interests receive hate over the internet, it's full of misogyny. Neither the paper nor I are saying it was misogyny *just* because it was hate aimed at women—no—it was hate which was very gender specific.

The paper quoted hundreds of people writing to female media interests, things like, "You stupid dumb bitch, I will rape you and your saggy cunt",

"Fucking ugly bitch, I will fucking kill you because you're too ugly to be raped", and so on. You see the ever-so-subtle misogyny?

In conclusion, the paper discovered that when hate is targeted towards men, it's very generic: "I hate you", "Delete your stupid fucking channel", things like that. But when women received hate, it was majority males and almost always sounded as if it was all coming from the same person. The hate women received was almost always referring to their bodies: being abused, raped, killed, or otherwise.

This research took place between 2010 and 2017. Forgive me for my broadness, I read a lot of papers in university and can barely remember my login for the student portal at this stage. My point is, this was very recent research about comments over social media. Anyone can understand and undertake that. All you have to do is search, observe, and be aware you might find something you don't like.

It was situations like this amongst others which made me realise all the anger I'd been missing out on. Can you believe how I felt? Years and years of being oppressed in certain situations, and I had no idea! Things I should've said "fuck off" to I simply laughed off. I will sort of admit this must go both ways and say that perhaps the people I should've said fuck off to also didn't realise they were being offensive. I mean, I didn't—and I'm a women. So how were they supposed to know? Not saying what they did was right; it just stresses my point about being researched in these matters. After all, knowledge is power and all that.

Here comes my main point about all these issues and being educated on them. When you picture a women's march in your head, what do you visualise? Angry people of all shapes, races, and sizes holding homemade signs displaying phrases such as "Anything You Can Do We Can Do Bleeding".

That's what I picture. See ... *here* is my issue. Do you see any males or otherwise in that image? No, I didn't think so. Now picture an anti-racism march, like for the Black Lives Matter movement. In my head there is similar imagery to that of the women's march: Angry people, but this time it's people of colour, men and women or otherwise, handmade signs still apply. This time their sign says things like "Until the Colour of Your Skin Is the Target You Will Never Understand". (Angela Davis said this.) See any white people here? Correct! Neither did I. In fact, in my head, this peaceful protest gets broken up by armed white police officers with tear gas.

But that's only because that's actually what happened recently in Minneapolis. A black man named George Floyd was brutally murdered by police because he was allegedly resisting arrest—while lying face-down in the gutter with an officer's knee on his neck for almost nine minutes. The internet has ignited with rage, as am I, leading to a protest today near the Third Police Precinct on Minnehaha Avenue. Some of George Floyd's last harrowing words were, "I can't breathe" (same last words of the late Eric Garner, a black horticulturist from New York also murdered by police in 2014—he was unarmed and outnumbered five to one. Evidence to support Floyd's case continues to grow, as well as attempts to disprove it. Some sources say he was a hero; others *do not* show him in such a flattering light. However, whatever one chooses to believe, it doesn't take away from the fact he died unlawfully, unnecessarily, with a knee pressing down on his neck for nine minutes whilst witnesses shouted, "Stop, you're killing him!"

Women's marches are there for men to hear. Marches in the name of race are targeted towards whites. Yet it would seem the very people these grand (potentially life-threatening) gestures are meant for are the only ones not listening. This is where the importance of education and the deadly repercussions of ignorance show their influence. It is the voices of angry people that will change history. If you're not angry, you're either ignorant or the oppressor—or both. The privileged never march or wish to change the world because why would they? They don't see the things that need changing.

Although I haven't had the chance yet to read *Why I'm no Longer Talking to White People about Race* by Reni-Eddo Lodge, I watched an insightful interview with her on YouTube, titled "What happens when I try to talk race with white people" (December 2017). She explains that when she was in a conversation about inequality and tried to bring up race, her conversation partner would automatically become defensive and accuse her of having a chip on her shoulder. I wonder, what do these people think of the late Floyd and Garner— would they be so flippant then?

So I guess if you ever find me talking about the injustice within society against the oppressed, or actor Tom Holland, please don't roll your eyes or tell me to be quiet. Instead, fucking listen. Learn.

It's 2020. We can still do better.

8

Surely All Those Lights Must Need a Break?

Whilst writing at my desk tonight, like I do most nights now, Georgia came home in an internally bad mood. I don't want to be disrespectful towards her and her family by exposing their business, so I shall keep this as brief as possible. One of her family members is fatally ill at the moment, and it's looking like the end is near. Georgia and her family received more bad news today, creating Georgia's internal anger. Georgia gets angry a lot; it's her kneejerk reaction to most things negative.

When she came home, I joined her in the kitchen, and we spoke about our days, comparing stories. I told her about how I brought a new toothpaste today only to find we already had an unopened one in the bathroom draw. She told me about the errands she ran with her aunt, preparing for her family member's passing—our stories were a little different in tone. She lay on my bed as I sat typing at my laptop, and I asked her questions about her family and how they were doing.

She then Face-Timed her mum to ask her something, but her little sister answered the call.

"I'll be there in twenty minutes", Georgia said and quickly hung up.

"Do you want me to come with?" I asked.

"Up to you, I don't mind". She shrugged.

"Your bullshit is my bullshit". I shrugged back, collecting both our packets of tobacco, filters, and papers from the coffee table.

Again, to respect their privacy, I won't say exactly what happened, but it led to Georgia and me, dressed in part clothes, part pyjamas, walking to their house at roughly 11 o'clock that night.

On our walk home, now around 1.35am, we joked a lot. Almost too much. I think with hindsight we were both trying to lighten our own moods. We spoke about buying vibrators and why company buildings kept their lights on all night. I said it was because it was cheaper to keep them on all the time than turn them off and on every day; Georgia did not think that was true and said, "Surely they must just need a break?"

We were exhausted. "Thanks for trekking with me, I guess", she said quietly.

"Your bullshit is my bullshit", I repeated. "It's part of the job".

She laughed and joked about how many times I'd have to join her in something like this before I gave up and handed in my best friend notice. We guessed around six times before I'd feel like this is just too much and not what I signed up for originally back in year 9.

We came home and made cups of tea, sat in our living room smoking roll-ups until around 03.30am. This is not how either of us predicted our night would've gone. In the time between getting home and going to bed, we spoke about death of all kinds. We spoke about the fact we were going to kill ourselves before either of our mothers died, ensuring we would never live to see the day. We spoke about the fact Georgia doesn't really have her dad in her life; we discussed how she'd feel if she found out he had passed away. I brought up the fact that unlike her, I do have a dad, two including my stepdad; we talked about the fact I wouldn't just mourn one father figure but both when those dreaded days came. People's last moments were brought up, and whether we thought death was painful. (I don't think it is; I think it's like falling asleep.)

We discussed whether it was better to die quickly, in a car crash, for example, or slowly, like a terminal illness. We both voted quickly. The idea of slowly accepting your fatal doom every day, getting weaker, more dependant, making others emotional is heartbreaking. Quite frankly Georgia and I are both similar in that we hate feeling like burdens, priding ourselves on our independence—I think if we found out we were terminally ill, we'd kill ourselves to save others the trouble of having to care for us. Although there can be cons for dying suddenly, such as what if the last thing you said to a loved one wasn't the *best* note to leave things on? At least when you know death is soon, you can fix arguments; clear the air. You can tell people you love them. If one second you're there and the next you're not, I hope that whatever I last said to the people I cared about was nice. God, I really do.

Our conversations ended with us staring into the abyss, in different directions, totally silent, looking through the smoke and rising sunlight in the room. I don't know what she was thinking about, I was thinking about my Dad passing away. He has a lot of health conditions and this global pandemic has elected him high risk, meaning he must take extra precautions to not catch the virus or he's done for. This constant reminder has inevitably made me unwilling think about his untimely death more than I ever have. I thought about how sad I'd be if he died and how it would break my heart. He is *my dad*. I felt a lump at the back of my throat and tears forming.

"Well, what a fucking gloomy note to end the night on", I said as I got up from the sofa, slapping Georgia on the leg as I did so.

"That's what I do", she replied, half joking.

I woke up the next day from a video call from

Georgia. She was out with her family. I was in bed. It was 2pm. In my defence, what else would I be doing during a pandemic? And we did go to bed very late. She told me that after we went to bed last night, she started writing using the notes app on her phone. She sent me what she wrote, and I told her I thought it was really good. I really did like what she wrote and felt somewhat responsible for her inspiration. Her style was similar to mine, with just a tad darker humour. I encouraged her to buy a laptop and start writing like me, but she declined. She said she didn't know how long this writing phase would last for her and felt that buying a laptop would be a waste of money.

I find it fascinating that highly emotional times in our lives force us to be more creative than usual—it's like humans' way of releasing extra energy. We write what we cannot contain in our heads, we draw what we can't express using words, we sing what we can't speak, and we use actions like dance to do the talking for us. It does make me wonder if emotions are harmful in a way. If someone feels too sad, they jump off a bridge. If someone loves too hard, they can become abusive. I'm not trying to normalise suicide or excuse domestic abuse; I just think the way humans act and feel is interesting. Slightly morbid. My passions make me stressed; my values make me angry; my sadness at one point rendered me paralysed. This just makes me think humans are too intelligent for our own good, too evolved to understand quite how to control certain aspects of our modern lifestyles.

Other mammals don't have racism, homophobia, or gender oppression. You don't see animals senselessly kill one another or see a couple that have mated for life abuse one another. Animals eat what satisfies them, never too much. Male birds do some sort of fancy show with pretty feathers to attract their mates—that's technically consent, right? I just feel like animals evolved enough to be able to live completely harmoniously. Yes, humans are intelligent and are able to accomplish some amazing goals, but perhaps knowledge isn't *always* power. Perhaps there is such a thing as knowing too much. In our constant advance in science, we are able to help families have children where they naturally couldn't; we've also developed things like nuclear weapons. Thanks to our science we were able to reach the moon (unless you believe it is all faked), and we have also developed the capacity to take images which show our planet dying every single day. Maybe Thanos from the Avengers movies had a point; perhaps we'd all be better off extinct.

For the past few days, Georgia has been out of the house a lot, which left me at home with Luna our cat. Like I said earlier, Luna was quite an independent cat but for the past few days at random points she enters my room, yells one loud "Meow!" in my direction, and then leaves the room. When I hear this singular meow, I turn round in my chair and ask her, "Yes? What do you want?" What does she want? She has food, water, and a clean litterbox. I stroke her for a little bit, but she just struts out of the room with no explanation. I wish I could talk to her. I wonder if she addresses me by a name in her head, like Mum or Food Dispenser. Maybe she just calls me The Small One. I am very short; she wouldn't be wrong.

Georgia came home just as I was leaving to walk to the corner shop. We desperately needed some oat milk and lemons. She came with me. On our way back, we witnessed a slight disturbance in the street. A women had left her car in the middle of the main road we lived on, creating a traffic jam; she was arguing loudly with a man outside his front door (I only presume it's his front door). I don't know about you, but this is not an uncommon sight for me. The areas I have grown up in have made me pretty desensitised to things like bar fights, public arguments, and police presence. Both the man and woman (still in heated argument) walked to the woman's car boot and started intensely squabbling —he was trying to close the boot whilst she was trying to open it. This led their argument to turn physical. I can't say for certain what happened as I was a little down the street at this point, but I'm almost certain she went for him *first,* which encouraged him to restrain her arms and hit her back. My eyes were fixated on this interaction, and when it turned to actual physical abuse, I shouted, "Georg, Georgia!" to gain her attention and get her to see what I was seeing.

"Why are you stopped and looking for? She's driven to his house, she's parked in the road, she started this whole thing—you can't blame him for this turning physical! What are you gonna do, just standing there watching?" Georgia shouted back.

"He *hit* her!" I retaliated. It would seem the couple's domestic had made me and Georgia have our own.

But she had a point. What was I going to do, just stand there? I don't think I have the courage to get involved, nor do I believe my involvement would actually help—it's also none of my business. Cars drove around the women's black Aldi to start the flow of traffic again. I guess if I was a witness and the police were called, I could tell them what actually happened in case one of them lied. That way the truth could be known. (Then again, snitches get stitches, so perhaps I wouldn't.) But the police were never called, and I have no idea what happened after the fight with the car boot. Was it all the woman's fault? Did he really need to hit her back? I'm aware men should be able to defend themselves, but perhaps the restraint was enough. He was a big, muscly fella. Around late 20s. Could he not just walk into his front door and lock it, avoiding all confrontation with the angry woman verbally and physically? I don't want to seem like I feel the woman in this situation is completely innocent, but I have no idea what she was so angry about. I guess this argument will always leave me in a flux state of 'it's none of my business' and 'but I need to know' mind-set.

Georgia and I returned to the flat in silence, and we ate dinner ignoring our argument in the street. It would seem sometimes shouting really doesn't solve anything.

Tonight on the news, I saw the government has

issued more lenient policies which allow people to sit in each other's gardens, with a maximum number of people being six. This means I can go see my mum. I am very happy about that. The next day I got up and went straight round to my mum's to sit in her garden. Charles was also home, and it felt like old times—the three of us together. We exchanged pleasantries, and Mum made us drinks of lemonade, fruit juice, ice, and frozen fruit. The sun was so warm, and the sky was the bluest I think I've ever seen it. It really didn't feel like England, more like Spain. Mum and Charles's garden is gorgeous; they love animals and nature. The back wall is lined with a grapevine. The grapes aren't ready yet, but it still looked pretty exotic. They have an array of plant pots all containing different plants and vegetables. Radishes were their newest addition. They have a huge pond filled with orange, white, and black goldfish. The garden was so green and luscious I can see why they were so proud of it.

It didn't take long for us to get back into our normal pattern. Mum and I discussed friends, family, latest hobbies, and such. Charles and I debated or had heated conversation about politics, society, or economics. Charles and I always argue about things like this; I don't think there has been a single thing we can agree on. This debate was the most heated of them all. It was about George Floyd's cruel murder and the rioting that followed, which is in its fourth day now and has spread to other cities such as Chicago. Like I said earlier, it is the voices of angry people that will change history. Malcom X once said, "Communicate with them using a language they understand. If their language is violence, use violence". I may be slightly paraphrasing and absolutely butchering this man's great words, but you get my point. These people were sick of being ignored and demanded that white people listen. Now, finally, they were getting the attention they so craved—necessary for justice. No justice, no peace.

Please note that I am not blind to the cons of rioting. Yes, some rioters and protestors are bad. Yes, a lot of damage to public property, cars, and innocent business owners' shops will occur. Yes, *some* protestors take advantage of the chaos, just as *some* police are good and do not abuse their authority. I do not condone rioters attacking innocents, and I do not agree with rioters acting violent towards *all* cops. With that being said, I do still support the protests. Please do not think I am ignorant to the misconduct from all sides of this equation. I would argue that although these *some-people* exist, they are not the majority of those that take part. Also, in the weeks following the protests and riots, a lot of progress was made in favour of the BLM cause and policing—showing *it does work.*

Charles said he thought that what happened to Floyd was merciless, evil, and completely avoidable. I guess I lied, because we both agreed on that. However, he didn't think the issue was with race and argued similar things must happen with white people too. This is what led to the shouting. I even swore at him. I do have a bit of a potty mouth, I'll admit. I use swear words a lot but never *at* anyone. Never with anger or bad intention, if that makes sense. However, this conversation with Charles got my so hyped up I actually said, "No way, you fucking liar!" To my own stepdad. What made me happy is that rather than telling me off, Charles and Mum simply brushed past it—clearly understanding I was just passionate. I know I'm technically an adult, but no one likes being told off by their parents at any age. Charles and I agreed to disagree, like normal. Mum mediated us, like usual. She never got involved, although whenever it does happen, she always gives me a *look* when I make a really good point which expresses her secret agreement with me.

Later on in my visit, I remembered I packed my new books to read if I got the chance. I packed all three as I wasn't too sure which one I'd be in the mood for. I prefer options. To wind Charles up, I got out *Why I'm no Longer Talking to White People about Race* and pretended to read it at the garden table.

Mum laughed hard at this. "*You* need to read that!" She gestured to Charles, still giggling.

Here is the surprising thing. Rather than laugh it off or getting annoyed, he agreed. He actually wanted to read it.

"May I have a look at that?" he asked.

"Yeah, yes of course", I replied. I was so happy and astonished at his request I spoke with the voice of a child. My attitude totally changed.

"She's a journalist, written for loads of publications. This is her first book", Charles explained to Mum, although she didn't actually ask him anything. "I can have it back to you by Monday if that's all right?" he asked me.

"Yeah! Go ahead. I have two more here I need to burn through anyway, so absolutely no rush! I hope it helps you understand more. Just please, Charles, please, don't bother reading it if you're not going to even try and hear others opinions on this stuff", I replied. Could he tell how I genuine I was being? How much this meant to me?

"Family book club!" Mum yelled excitedly. Mum can be quite a joker at times.

It might not mean a lot to you, and you may not even understand how serious that whole interaction was, but I hope you do. I like to believe every family has a slightly racist/homophobic/ prejudiced member (sometimes more than one). If you do, you'll know it's basically impossible to change his or her opinions, and so often just give up and say, "Yes, Grandad, yes, you've said this before, we know. 'Gays are wrong'. OK, we get it", whilst rolling your eyes. At this point you have accepted they're just too old to change.

Charles turns 61 in July. I know better than anyone he can say problematic things and not have the most up-to-date values or beliefs (he is a boomer, after all), but when he asked to read my book, I felt a sudden wave of appreciation and respect for him. It was something I thought someone of his age and cultural standpoint would never have done. It made me feel like something I said had gotten through. Perhaps he was willing to listen and change. I don't know what he thinks of the book yet, he might hate it, but I will never forget the fact he read it anyway. It felt like I was finally being heard, which meant so much. It also made me feel better as a white person, spreading the word of white privilege and educating those not-so-woke. This was my way of showing solidarity for those protesting in the states. This was my way of saying, "I stand with you", from across the pond.

9

Working in Retail Should Be like Jury Duty

I came home from Mum and Charles's, had a bath, and reheated a shepherd's pie, which Georgia brought home for me from her aunt's the other night for dinner.

Georgia came home a little later and sat on my bed whilst I typed at my desk; we exchanged stories of our days, like usual. I told her how I'd called Charles a fucking liar, and she told me about her family and her very ill family member. She asked if she could borrow my copy of *Why I'm no Longer Talking to White People about Race* after Charles was done with it and I gladly said yes. It seemed I would make activists out of these two stubborn people eventually (not that Georgia needed the white privilege lesson). Despite not having actually read it yet, I felt listened too. She told me she had no desire to read my other two, however, which is fine. I wasn't going to push it.

During this conversation our doorbell rang, and it was our dear friend Grace. Grace, Georgia, and I were somewhat of a dynamic trio throughout school and college. Over the better part of a decade, our threesome went through some ups and downs, but we always came back together eventually. Deep down I think everyone hates Grace, for good reason: She is absolutely beautiful. Not 'pretty' or even just attractive—but absolutely, flawlessly, naturally beautiful. She comes from a good, beautiful looking family—her parents are goals of what one would want for a twenty-five-plus-year marriage. She has a cool older brother, even cooler middle sister, and is the favourited youngest of the three. Her house is big and well decorated with a garden that has the ability to host the best bonfires and BBQs. She always has dogs, lots and lots of dogs. She is smart, hardworking, funny, kind, generous, thoughtful, and non-judgmental. It's impossible for us to go out without her saying hello to at least five strangers, and we always joke that she must know everyone in Portsmouth. She was always abundantly liked throughout school and college, completely uncontroversial or unargumentative.

I'm not saying Grace is perfect—she has flaws like everyone—but she is pretty damn close. Everyone deep down hates Grace because no one can find a bad word to say about her, her background, or lifestyle. During the span of this lockdown, Grace has delivered to Georgia and me homemade mermaid cupcakes, Costa coffee, and today she dropped off some homemade strawberry jam her nan made. (I had it on toast the next day. Very tasty!) Grace told me she had some clothes for me if I wanted them. They didn't fit her anymore and she thought I'd like them. See? Fucking bitch. So damn fucking nice.

I think I might do something for Grace now, since she has gone above and beyond for us both this pandemic. I might buy her a present and drop it off to her door sometime this week. I think she'd like that. I should probably run this by Georgia; she likes that sort of thing too. (Later I asked Georgia, and she told me she had given Grace some money for petrol, so it would seem this is a solo mission. I sent her some eyebrow tint in the post a few days later. She loved it.)

I spent the rest of the night writing in my room whilst Georgia sat in the living room watching videos on Facebook. She sent me posts about the George Floyd riots via Instagram to keep me in the loop. I finished writing about 2am and went to bed.

I woke up today and felt so pointless. I think it's week ten of quarantine now. I really don't know. I know it started a day or two before Georgia's 21st birthday—which is 22 March. The date today is 30 May. I've heard a lot of news about possibly returning to work on the fifteenth of June, so I'll see, perhaps this day-in, day-out nothingness will come to an end soon.

I currently work for a shop in a retail park called Gunwharf Quays. I really like my job here; I think it's my favourite job I have ever had. I've worked for a lot of shops as a retail sales assistant since I was 16 and know how bad this kind of work can be. There was the supermarket, which I mentioned earlier, but there was also a concession I worked for in Debenhams, a well-to-do brand which made me wear one of their dresses as uniform, a brand which I left after a month because one of the other employees made it her life's mission to make my life hell (her name was Isabell, and she was a massive dick), and one job in a call centre which is actually the only job I have ever been fired from. It was one of the happiest days of my working life because I really hated that job. These jobs are good because they're easy to an extent; you clock in, do the job, and leave.

Sometimes they can be very hard mentally. Beside the abuse from customers (of which one does become desensitised to after a while, you learn just how stupid the general public can be and start laughing at them when they get mad), they can be quite toxic places of work. Students such as I are forced to choose between employment or our education—pressured into working above our contracted hours because they need the extra pair of hands. Why hire someone else when they can get 16- to 20-year-olds to do the same job for cheaper? We're often the ones also guilt-tripped into covering shifts, as anyone older than us will pull out the classic, "Well, I *can't* do my Tuesday ten to four shift because I have a *child*", excuse. Alright, I get it, you're a working mother, but Jesus Christ, I'm *not,* so why is your kid my fucking problem now? I have to take a class! They never even asked nicely, which was the worst bit. They just had the entitlement of their parental responsibilities to keep them justified.

These types of workplaces are always filled with dodgy workplace romances and gossip. "Wow they fucked in the stockroom? No way, gross!" or "Oh my God, did she really just speak to you like that? She's not even a manager; she's just a sales assistant!"

I've always wanted someone to make a TV show similar to *The Office* about retail. I think it would be brilliant and exactly what we need. I also always say every single person (no matter their background or lifestyle—just anyone) should work in retail for at least two weeks in their lifespan. I think they should get a letter posted through their door calling them to do their time, kind of like jury duty.

I think this is necessary because you can definitely tell those people who have never worked customer service and those who have.

"Why is the till broke? Unacceptable!"

Really, bitch? You think I did this? You think I wanted my till to break, to gain what? I'm just as annoyed as you!

"Hello, I've looked around your whole store, and I really like this dress, but do you have it in any other colours?"

Fuck off! *Do you see that dress in any other colours? What, you just think I have a blue, green, and red one out back that can only be accessed if you ask a member of staff? No! What you see is what I fucking have.*

"Excuse me, but I don't suppose you have any more of these out back?" or "Is there not something you can find to fix the till out back?"

I don't know what the fuck some customers think we have stored away out back, but let me tell you, in all my years of working in retail (five and counting), in almost every store I have worked in, 'out back' consists of staffs' bags, coats, phones, lunches, a microwave, a kettle, cups, a sink, a chair or two to sit on, a first-aid kit, and a hoover. Yes, sometimes we have stock as well, but if I say, "No,

I'm sorry, that's the last of our stock", don't fucking ask me to check out back because I fucking know what's out there. I walk past it every shift. Phew. I could probably write a whole book on retail alone, but don't worry, I won't just yet. Just know that most retail assistants fucking hate you, and we hate it when you *tell us how to do our jobs*. Fucking clock in if you know so damn much.

Anyway, I really like my job in Gunwharf. My manager understands that I have (or at least had) university work to be getting on with and didn't force me to do overtime when I was stressed. There is no gossip, not really, and we all get on pretty well. There are no workplace romances, thank God. Well, none anyone knows about. If there are, then good job for keeping them so under wraps, guys (Olly and Gavin, I'll bet it's you). The pays all right, the hours aren't bad, and 90 per cent of the customers are super understanding. In fact, I enjoy my job a little too much. Sometimes I think I could work there forever. Clock in, do my job, go home. Simple, happy life. The idea of working in a shop forever doesn't sound *too bad*, but I always wanted something a little more for myself. I want to do *things*. Meaningful things. I don't want to just work in a shop forever. What kind of impact on the world is that? I don't mean to be rude to those that work in shops for what seems like forever. I really don't. I just want something bigger than myself; you can understand that, can't you? I like the idea that on my deathbed I can say I changed something, made the world a better place, and so on. Perhaps I am being very optimistic and a little arrogant. I hope it doesn't come across that way, although I kind of hear it myself.

If you told me around ten weeks or so ago I'd be locked in my flat with no one but Georgia and the cat, I probably would've spent my time doing better things. I feel like I've wasted a lot of time. I could've started yoga, gone for runs (I went on one and felt like an idiot), read more, watched more, and so on. I've procrastinated a lot. I am constantly hit with a wall every time I wake up in the afternoons (yes you heard me correct, afternoons). Time doesn't feel real anymore. Days and nights consist of the same thing: *nothing.*

I've heard a lot about the rise in domestic and child abuse since lockdown started. This hits me with the hard realisation that a lot of people don't live happy home lives and need the escape of school and work to actually *survive.* I was aware of these issues before but not the severity of it all. Older people are struggling more than usual too, being quarantined worse than younger, fitter people due to their high risk. I guess I should probably stop complaining and be grateful for the ten-ish weeks paid leave from work locked away with my best mate and pet. I really don't have a position to complain.

Grace's grandad passed away from COVID-19 about a month ago. Now that's a family which have really suffered due to this pandemic. It is interesting watching society during times like this, 'warlike' conditions, as some have referred it to. We're confronted with grand acts of kindness, like how thousands of retired NHS workers have returned to work, along with not yet 'qualified' student nurses, to help with the sick in hospitals. Royal Mail employees have dressed up in 'silly' costumes to brighten up they days of people during their rounds. On top of everything else, supermarkets have set aside designated hours for the elderly to do their shopping in peace, whilst giving NHS staff discounts. It is really beautiful to see.

I even tried to do *my* bit. I posted handwritten notes to the other three flats in my building, telling them that if they needed any help with shopping and things, they could call me (since I am a young, non-high-risk person with no dependants) and I'd assist. Only one person replied, my neighbour George. He texted me and thanked me for my kind gesture and wished me well. That was really wholesome.

I guess just like absolutely everything in the universe, there are opposites. Two sides to every coin. One on side, for instance, you see the kindness in people. On the other, there's evil in people such as domestic abusers. Situations like this exaggerate these sides to make them more visible than ever before. There were always kind people in the world, just as there will always be evil. Just with humans with heightened emotions get creative, it would seem during times of heightened chaos people also act towards things that are bigger than themselves. It is things like this that makes me fully support the rioting going on in America right now. The worse the issue, the bigger the rebellion. The sadder the situation, the bigger acts of kindness are shown. I don't really know what I'm trying to say right now, but I guess just as all things, the actions of humans follows Isaac Newton's third law—for every action, there is an equal and opposite reaction. No matter if it's good or bad.

10

I'm off to Church in the Morning

This isolation has given one a lot of time to reflect on being single. Time away from people and dating has given me a little perspective on things. After my break-up with Leech, and some much-needed time alone (nine months, apparently), I started dating again. These dates weren't to gain another relationship status, they were just kind of … fun. I went into them fully expecting to either never hear from them again, maybe go on a second date, sleep with them, or all three. This process of trial and error allowed me to feel very empowered, and the act of not really giving a shit helped me disconnect from love in *that* way. I dated men and women. Some were shy, some were blunt, some were cocky, and few I really liked. What I will say is that I didn't really gain a lot from any of these dates, but I didn't lose anything either. They just killed some time.

Looking back, I suppose it's not very nice to view people as 'time killers', but then again I think that's how they viewed me right back. A wild oat to sow. Despite all these encounters (there were quite a few, I think my body count is almost double digits), I'm a romantic at heart. I love all that *Notebook* shit. The idea of finding a lover, best friend, and partner in one singular person—a soul mate—is very appealing to me. (Of course good luck trying to compete with Georgia. She gets very jealous.)

My relationship with Leech outlined everything I *didn't* want in a soul mate. I didn't want a man- or woman-child. I don't want to do all your dishes, cook all your meals, be your therapist to your every inconveniences when you're never mine, be your breadwinner, and be a piece of meat. I want a partnership, an alliance, two strong forces that equally aid each other. The idea is to add towards one another, not always or exclusively take. Leech was more like the son I never asked for than the other half I so craved. It was so draining.

This has led me to have incredibly high standards when it comes to finding a new partner and is making me think that what I want doesn't really exist. I might be doomed to be a crazy cat lady forever. As soon as they mentioned they weren't so good with finances and had no intention to stop relying on their parents, I crossed them off. As soon as they said they weren't in a 'very good place', and seeing me was the only good thing in their life at the moment, I crossed them off. I have no issue helping people with mental health issues, but a women you've gone on a few dates with shouldn't be your saviour—I am not here to heal you. You need to heal yourself (possibly with the help of professionals or loved ones). If I'm your only source of happiness, please note that is not what I signed up for. That is not the massive responsibility a partner should have. I should be one of the things that make you happy or help you, not the only thing. If someone constantly repeated, "Let's just go back to my place", I crossed him off. I have no problems with casual sex, but Jesus, I'm not that easy. They'd probably skip the foreplay and pump in and out for four minutes and then roll over and fall asleep. Think that's really worth my time? C'mon. If they spoke about themselves a lot and didn't ask me enough of the right questions, I'd cross them off. Don't just ask me how many people I've slept with and what it's like to sleep with a girl. Ask me about my hobbies and interests. If they seemed too quiet, I knew we had no future. I understand people get nervous, but I'm not here dressed in my nicest smart-casual outfit to view the silent movie which is you. Have some personality, you're on a date! So here I was, crossing off people left, right, and centre in my head. Nope. Not you. Not you either. Nah. I'm fully aware there were things about me all these people didn't like, and that's completely fine. If you don't like my sense of humour or the fact I wear a lot of make-up, that's okay. I wish you all the best, you'll find someone you like, and I'll find someone that likes me.

My dates became weekly entertainment updates with my friends and co-workers. There was the 'Aha, literally' guy, where his only reply to everything I said would be a brief laugh followed by the word literally. There was 'Polish', who was Polish. This nickname wasn't meant in disrespect, it was just the only factor which was different compared to the others. He was nice. One of my favourites. I'll never forget the time we finished having sex and I asked him, still panting, "So, what are you up to tomorrow?" and he replied, "Oh, I'm off to church in the morning".

There was Dafro, which is a mixture of the names 'Daddy' and 'Afro'. I'm not too sure where the Daddy bit came from, I think that was Patrick's doing, but the afro bit is self-explanatory. I really liked Dafro, only he stood me up to get back with his ex-girlfriend. Joke's on him though, because it obviously didn't go very well as I received a "Hey x" over Snapchat about two weeks later. I ignored it, of course. He should've realised my value before, not after.

None of the women did or said anything in particular to earn a nickname. One was very shy, another not over her ex, one was very pleasant, but I just didn't find her that attractive in person—although she was beautiful, she just wasn't my type. All in all, I'm a dating expert now. I have the small talk nailed, know how to dress for any type of date, and can seal the deal pretty well (if I do say so myself—I haven't had any complaints). Now I feel like I've done all that can be done and am instead going to sit back and let my soul mate find me. No more dates. No more Tinder. I'm bored of it all. The act of going on a date isn't special to me anymore, which is a bit sad. I've kind of ruined it for myself. From now on I'm going to just do me: go to work, see my friends, spend time with family, and work on my hobbies. If someone comes along, fine. If someone doesn't, also fine. This really takes the weight off my shoulders. I think I am going to read

The Unexpected Joy of Being Single now. It seems appropriate.

Now feels like a good time to talk about tattoos. Why? Why not, it's my book.

I have six tattoos and counting. One on each thigh, three on my right arm, and one on my lift wrist. I love tattoos and almost have a full sleeve. I think after my right arm is finished I'll start one on my left. My mum and pretty much my whole family hates tattoos, especially mine. "No! What have you gone and done now!" they ask. "What about when you get older?" or "I like tattoos but *not* on women". The usual. It upsets me that they don't like them, but not enough to stop getting them done. I don't even mind if they choose to not be tattooed, which most of them haven't, but still, please don't yell at me for it. I don't think any of them have actually asked me what I have. I have two portraits of famous fictional people, a Tardis from the TV show *Doctor Who*, an animal piece (made up of a stag, fox, and wolf), a wolf on its own, and a linework rose on my left wrist. Every single one has a meaning to it, a very deep special significance to me. I'm not going to explain each one and what it means because I don't really want to. Not a single person has asked—they don't want to know. That hurts the most. But if no one asked, why should I tell them anyway? I didn't get them done for others, I got them for me. That, I guess, is how they'll stay.

Why should I care what they will look like when I'm elderly? In my head, I picture the most kick-ass grandmother around. Mug *me* will you, gang of teenagers? Fuck right off. I don't think it makes me look less feminine. I think I'm just a women with pictures on my skin. I can still dress feminine in a dress and heels, or I can dress how I usually do in my jeans and T-shirt. Tattoos don't stop that.

"What about jobs?" people ask. Hopefully my answer to this will always be the same, and it's this: if an employer looks at harmless pictures on my skin and makes that the *only deciding factor* which doesn't give me the job, then I don't want to work there anyway. Imagine working for such a behind-the-times institution? Who judges people for having tattoos? Laughable. I didn't spend all this money and all that time in pain just to hide them, so I'll just work for companies that appreciate my skills and don't make me hide who I am, thanks. As I said before, I am four foot eleven and weigh about forty-nine kilograms. If you see me and think gangster, drug addict, criminal, or anything similar just because of my tattoos, you're an idiot. I'm the size of a child and incredibly well mannered. For God's sake, one of my tattoos is a Tardis—hardly a prison tattoo. Or a Nazi symbol. Now *that's* a tattoo I'd understand you to discriminate against.

I have been tattooed by a few tattoo artists, not just one. I love all different styles of art and therefore go to an array of artists—they are all just so damned talented! I think people who have never met or seen tattoo artists think they're rude, inhumane, and downright crazy. Please allow me to educate you. Tattoo artists are *the* nicest, smartest, most liberal, honest, trustworthy people I have ever met. If I could draw, I'd bang every single tattoo shop owners door until I got an apprenticeship.

When I was living in Brighton, I met one named Dolly. This isn't her legal first name but instead her self-identified tattoo name, I guess. I never asked her about it. Anyway, Dolly's artwork was incredible. It was nice to see her glamourous pink, overly feminine designs. She tattooed a lot of references to the film *Mean Girls,* which I loved (fun fact: my dissertation for my BA degree was on *Mean Girls*). Dolly, however, was stunningly dark and edgy. She was a walking contradiction, and I was a big fan of it. She had long jet-black hair, a striking face with dark features, wore a lot of black, and was a slim-curvy built woman. She walked with purpose, spoke with authority, and had a really welcoming way she'd speak to her clients. As much as I'd never want to be on Dolly's bad side, I also knew I could ask her any question about tattooing and she'd answer with respect, knowledge, and kindness. She made me feel very comfortable and never made me feel silly for asking for a break from the pain. Dolly did both of my thigh pieces, and I can say with confidence I don't see them fading anytime soon; she really drilled in those colours. It is with meeting Dolly was I taught about the lifestyle of a tattoo artist.

"I bet it must be so cool being a tattoo artist, drawing for a living", I said to her naively. I could tell from the look on Dolly's face she wasn't in agreement, but she knew I didn't mean any harm by what I said. I just didn't understand at the time.

"Sometimes", she replied bluntly.

"Oh. Why is it not so good sometimes? Must be stressful being self-employed I'll bet". I tried to save myself.

"Yeah, when people cancel, they don't understand they're cancelling me from paying my bills. Sometimes people don't listen to my aftercare advice and end up ruining my work, things like that", she explained.

Whilst we were talking, and Dolly tattooed, an apprentice named Lewis looked over Dolly's shoulder, observing her technique.

"Hey, feel free to sit at the end of the bed if you like and watch from there. I don't mind", I said to Lewis. With that, Lewis and Dolly roared in laughter.

"Me? Sit down? No, No! That is very kind of you, though" Lewis replied.

"He can't sit down. Actually, Lewis, can I have a tea please?" Dolly asked, more telling Lewis to make her a tea than asking.

I asked why he wasn't allowed to sit.

"When I was an apprentice, I cleaned my boss's car every day for two weeks in the snow. I ran errands. Cleaned the shop from top to bottom even when it wasn't dirty". Dolly huffed. "If you can't go through hell to learn how to tattoo, you clearly don't want it enough. There are lots of other people who want to be in your position".

This was when I realised just how amazing tattoo artists are. They earned their chairs, their reputations, through years of hell. Apparently, it can take up to a year in an apprenticeship to even pick up a tattoo gun in some shops. The tattoo artists were a little mean to Lewis, but not because they didn't like him (turns out Lewis and Dolly were friends before, and she got him the apprenticeship) but because that's their 'rite of passage'. You gotta respect that. This isn't just something Lewis went through; this is common practice amongst the tattoo industry. They don't teach tattooing in schools, so you got to go learn from an already-qualified tattoo artist—their way. Their rules.

One of the reasons I love tattoos and tattoo culture is the pain. No, I'm not a masochist. I just think it's quite profound suffering for something you love. If *Doctor Who* really means that much to me, I'll suffer four hours with Dolly to prove how much. If you love the idea of tattooing so much, you must suffer verbal and mental abuse with long hours and hard labour to even come close to a tattoo gun. The way I see it, if you have lots of visible, large tattoos, I'm not afraid of you. I do not fear you. I do not think less of you, I actually think way more. I respect that, man. I hear you; I see you. You've covered yourself with the names of those you love, images of the things you are inspired by, and created a new skin for yourself to expose your own identity. You took those needles and said,

"Fuck the patriarchy!" and I have no choice but to support you in that.

If you don't want tattoos, that's absolutely fine. They're permanent, painful, and possible to get infected if not done correctly. I get it, I really do. I just hope the next time you see someone with tattoos, you don't think less of them. They're creatives. They're artists. They appreciate art. They're deep. Someone can be a murderer and not have a single tattoo. Someone can be in a gang and be covered in tattoos. Judge someone on their mind-set, actions, values, and beliefs (if they're harmful to another's existence), but don't just judge them on their tattoos—that's their new skin. Tattoos are part of them now. Stop telling people they're wrong for getting them just because you don't like them. People with tattoos don't approach 'blank skinned' people and say, "Oh, how gross and plain!" We didn't ask for your rude opinion. Don't tell people they can only have the job if they cover the tattoos on their arms; what does that actually change? If you say that tattoos are unprofessional and although *you* don't mind them they might make the company look bad, just shut the fuck up and admit you're on the side of being judgmental.

11

Sticking My Big Nose to the Man!

I really want a nose job. In fact, I want a few cosmetic procedures done. I would like lip filler in my top lip because it is pretty much non-existent. My bottom lip is fine. This significant difference in size makes my life very difficult when wearing lipstick, it looks like a child has secretly gone through her mother's make-up bag. I want to start getting Botox injections when I'm around 25 or 27 years old. This is to prevent the development of wrinkles. Apparently, people who do this look youthful way into their 60s. I want to sort out my slight underbite, because it makes my chin invisible—I want a chiselled jaw like the models. Lastly, a good old-fashioned nose job. I feel like my nose is far to 'sticky-outy', and to add insult to injury, it has a large bulbus end.

Out of all four procedures, the nose job is the one I want the most; the other three I could give or take. I suppose my lips suit my face. I guess wrinkles will just make me look natural and distinguished. I know my jawline is only noticed by me. Since I was a teenager I have had a constant argument with myself in my head about my future nose job (officially called a rhinoplasty). Do I need to change it? Will I simply die if it doesn't change? No, not really. I have had my fair share of attention from people who obviously thought I was attractive, so it can't be *that bad*. Am I still a feminist if I get a nose job? What happened to sticking it to the man? "I will not conform to your idealised beauty standards!" we say. If I get this nose job, what does that say about me? Should I need to undergo surgery to feel pretty? Doesn't seem natural.

Yet, I don't feel pretty. My confidence has improved since I was a teenager but not enough to change my mind about the nose job. On the other hand, feminism should be about women making their own choices; being able to do what they want. So is it okay I get a nose job? God, this is hard. I don't want to go against my words by getting one. I really don't like sounding like a hypocrite. I also don't like the fact my nose is just a nose, yet society has told me it's *wrong*. Women get enough hate for their cosmetic changes (and their natural looks) as it is. "Her fake boobs don't even look nice, they're gross!", "Her lips look like a fish, I wouldn't be caught kissing those", and so on. I don't agree with the hate even if I also don't necessarily like the result of the surgeries.

I am not a fan of big boobs myself; I am a small titty fan I'll admit, but if you want a size DD+, for example, you should be able to go ahead, and I wish you the very best. I won't tell you they're gross, because beauty is in the eye of the beholder. What I would find attractive is your confidence and higher self-esteem for getting them done. Damn. Nothing hotter than a women who is *feeling herself* (like Beyoncé). It does make me wonder: Are all these procedures (good or otherwise) just the result of years of women being held at a higher expectation of 'pretty'? Like if I turned up to a job interview clean, presentable, and professional but had no make-up on, would that be polished enough for them? I don't think it would be. (Whilst I am writing this, I am awaiting the arrival of Florence Given's debut book *Women Don't Owe You Pretty [2020]*). I hope it holds the answers I desperately need.)

So, anyway, by this logic, as long as I do not hate on women or otherwise for their cosmetic surgeries (which I don't, or at least hope I don't), then it should be okay for me to get my nose job. I spoke to my mum about it a few weeks ago. I told her I found a clinic and did my research on it. I said that as soon as COVID-19 was under control, I'd be booking my appointment. She understood and even offered to help pay for it, to which I said she didn't have to. I did accept her offer to be dropped off and picked up from the clinic as it is located in Southampton and I don't drive. A driving licence was one of the big milestone things I had planned for this spring or summer, but of course that has all been called to a halt for now. Nonetheless, it was nice to know Mum wouldn't be angry about her only daughter drastically changing the way she looks—I guess compared to the tattoos, this is much better. Amazing. I'm morally in the clear. I think. Although, I suppose I'm biased about this. I think no matter how strongly someone feels about a topic, her own vanity and selfish needs will always prevail. It takes true courage and strength to put your cause before anything else. I guess I'm not that person … so I apologise to those who are disappointed in me when or if I undergo a nose job. Truly, I do not feel like my activism and values should be trampled by a simple rhinoplasty—but if you feel like it does, fair enough. I see your point. I just want to look in the mirror and feel happy about what I see, and I hope you can understand.

I do sometimes think about life post-rhinoplasty. Will I tell everyone? Will I leave them to figure it out for themselves? I guess I won't know until it's done. I hope people don't call me fake or any mean things. I hope my friends support me. I do consider myself quite an independent person; I do not tend to rely on others for a lot—in fact, I have it ingrained within me since childhood to never rely on anyone for anything if I can help it.

Despite all this training since childhood, I need a little emotional support just like anyone. I am no different from anyone else in the fact no one likes the idea of people being mean to them. It has occurred to me writing this that I want to change my nose to make myself feel better but care an awful lot about what others will think about it. Perhaps I am unknowingly changing my nose for them as well. God, my brain hurts from the possibilities. Perhaps this is what another issue of feminism is, women's inability to win. If I don't get my nose job I may be considered ugly; if I get my nose job I will be considered fake. *I'm not naturally pretty.* "She's only hot now because she got that nose job, you should've seen her before!"

It seems the only winners here are the Graces of the world. Not only is Grace beautiful in face, hair, body, and personality, she never drags others down. She comments supportive emojis on my selfies, tells me I look nice or that my make-up is pretty, or she likes my nails. God, fuck you, Grace! Stop being practically perfect in every way. She also drives; fucking bitch even got her damn licence at 17 or 18 years old. Unbelievable.

Yet here I am, trying to do my fucking best with what I was born with and not doing very well with it. Whilst I sit here and type and think and type I am starting to develop a mind-set that someone out there in the world is not going to like something about you, so you might as well do what you want. That way, at least you're happy. You can't please everyone, so stop trying. Just make sure you're happy.

But of course that's a lot easier said than done.

Now, all I need is £5000 and I'll be sorted. Piece of cake. I'll think of you haters when Tom Holland and I are sipping wine over dinner on our 1st-year wedding anniversary. A girl can dream.

Speaking of mean people, did I ever tell you I went to an all-girls secondary school? I know I haven't yet, but it sounded like a nice transition. As much as I believe in the extraordinary creation that is the female form—Goddamn girls can be fucking vile. I mean really, from experience, I'd rather get beaten up and hospitalised by a group of boys than sit in a room with the popular girls from school for ten minutes. I remember things these girls would say, how they knew how to hurt someone with their venomous words. They'd get super personal, really descriptive, and it would never end. How I didn't witness more suicides in secondary school I have no idea. I'm glad to say the people who received their brute force were stronger than I imagined. I hope they're doing all right now, although it wouldn't surprise me if some of the things these girls said still follow them around today.

Not just words; these girls knew how to fight. Hair pulling, kicking, slapping—the odd one even punched well. My school wasn't like any movie you've probably seen about high school. If there was a movie about it, I think it would categorise as a psychological horror. What's scary about that is that this time I'm not trying to exaggerate for comic effect. It was the type of school where even the teachers were scared of some of the students. The best way to survive was head down and keep quiet. I feel like I did all right with this action plan.

My group of friends and position within the society of our school was the classic inbetweener ideology. Not the cool ones. Not a bunch of losers. Got our work done, but wasn't classified with the 'boffins'. Again, another example of how one can never win. It's funny looking back, because I think the rest of us all looked at the popular kids with disgust, dislike, and disregard. No one actually *liked* them; they all just liked each other. And they were scary. They ruled by fear, not with love. In theory, they weren't popular at all. If they were burning in a fire, no one, not even the boffins, would piss on them. Now they are a group of stereotypical Vicky Pollards. I've lost count of how many have had a baby before the age of 20. Not that that's inherently a bad thing (I'm sure most of them are all right parents), but I will say it does not surprise me a single bit.

Bringing these two points together, I think I'll worry more about what women think about my nose job over men. I think men will just look at me and say "Ah, nose job? Fair enough. Did it hurt?", whilst women will think all sorts of things. I think out of anger, jealousy, or just flat-out judgment they will not take too kindly to my nose job and say things like, "Yeah, but why, Mayg? Your nose wasn't *that bad* before", slightly sniggering.

Maybe I'm wrong, it could well be that my long time around mean girls has conditioned me to think incorrectly about my own gender. Maybe not. I'm not saying whatever they will or won't say is going to change whether I undertake the surgery. I just think sometimes it is women who bring down other women. It's not just with my nose job I haven't even got yet, it's other things too.

"Have you put on weight?"

"Have you lost weight?"

"You look tired".

"You're so pale".

"Your foundation doesn't match your neck, hon".

"Are those shoes too big for you?" and so on.

In fact, I have more likely said these things to another. I am going to try to stop from now on. Not so others can stop telling me I'm tired and pale (they wouldn't be wrong, I'm basically blue in skin tone), but there's no need to, is there? I wonder how harmful my 'harmless' comments have been to some people? For an array of reasons, women cannot win. Trans people cannot win. Nonbinary cannot win.

"But you don't *look* like a man"

"I don't get it. You have a bra on?"

We can't win in a lot of ways but when it comes to looks. I feel like this is an issue completely avoidable and easily fixed. Just leave each other be. I saw a very interesting post on Twitter the other day, I believe it was called the "ten-second rule". If someone can't fix something in ten seconds, like fix their hair or get food from their teeth, don't mention it. You can say, "Oh, hey, your zip is undone!" but don't say, "Wow you have really big ears, huh?" This is something I will be implementing in my life; I hope you do too.

Something I always try to do is compliment people because I know how nice it is when I receive compliments. If I see something I think is pretty or new, I don't just think it, I mention it. "New bag? Girl, good taste" "Oh you've got new eyeshadow on; it looks great with your eye colour!" "Hey, Devon, I know you've been to the gym a lot recently, and I can see your efforts have paid off; good job!"

I notice how little we really give out compliments. I swear to God, someone told me my eyeliner was 'on fleek' in a club bathroom about three years ago, and honestly, I'm still riding that high. When I was sat in the cemetery before going to Milly's house, a woman stopped me and told me she loved the necklace I was wearing. It made me feel so good. Little did she know I was a little self-conscious about that necklace because it's quite out there; the fact she stopped a stranger and just gave that out for free was really fucking nice. Thank you, Graveyard Lady.

C'mon ladies, trans, and nonbinaries, we go through enough shit from men and the patriarchy; let's not be each other's enemies as well. It's tiring. Raise each other up! Say nice things! Speak kindness into existence. If you say ugly things and project your insecurities on to other people, you're no different from the popular girls in my secondary school. Instead, work on yourself, baby girl. Be your own biggest fan. Speak your beauty into the outside. I promise it's there. Compliment yourself, do a face mask, buy yourself a £45 candle from TX Maxx. It's called self-care. Good luck if you're ever on fire and need someone to pee on you. It is this in which I can do better as well.

Disclaimer: I do not endorse being mean to men either. I love men; I really do. This disclaimer is mostly aimed at cisgender males. I know it must be very anxiety inducing when people call you noodle arms, dad bod, or lanky. I can appreciate how annoying it must be to not be the right height or weight, or have the size of your penis referred to unnecessarily and making you feel emasculated. I also understand that I am not a man and therefore don't understand what it is like to be one, but please note I am aware you must have your own issues and complaints. Just because you're men does not make them less important. This chapter also doesn't mean *all* men are disrespectful to women or otherwise on how they look. This does *not* take away from the fact, however, that men are societal oppressors, and just like white people must accept their privilege, men must also acknowledge theirs. Because as author Reni Eddo-Lodge said, "You can choose not to see the sky, but it exists". You can treat women or otherwise well, and you may have had a hard life, but your life has not been made harder by your gender or the sex you were born with.

School wasn't just a dark time because of the popular girls. It was rough all round. In my last year at school, the year 11s had a hall to themselves for lunch. I sat on a table with a group of around fifteen other students in one large friendship group. I remember so vividly looking around at each girl and thinking, *Depressed, suicidal, eating disorder, abusive homelife, suicidal, eating disorder, you're all right but a bit weird, abusive relationship, drug addict …*

It dawned on me: we were all a bit fucked up. Most of them had been depressed at some point since I knew them, about a third had actually attempted suicide or self-harmed, two missed a year of school because of their eating disorders (they had to go spend time at some special clinic), and nearly all of us had sex before the age of consent. Saying we were fucked up might be a slight understatement. We all needed professional help! What's even stranger is that this type of behaviour, lifestyle, or mental health were so normalised it was actually unusual to be fine or normal. If you were fine, you were seen as hiding something. If you were fine, you were just rubbing it in to everyone else that they weren't so fine.

Looking back, 90 per cent of the people I went to school with were so tough by age 16. We would have mental breakdowns in the corridors, we'd be each other's therapists, and 13 year olds would force feed their friends lunches if they saw they missed their breaktime snack. We learned how much medical attention was required on self-harm cuts depending on how deep they were. ("That won't need stitches, Beth's went way deeper than that and hers healed okay without them".) We took each other to the sexual health clinics after school, sneakily getting the contraceptive pill and free condoms.

As much as girls can be mean, vile, and bullies—I also witnessed (and participated in) some genuinely life-saving acts of kindness. Thinking about this now has brought a lot back. I cannot believe how much we all dealt with at school, being minors, behind every adult's back. We'd sneak out the house at night, obtain contraband, lie, cheat, lie some more. We hung out with boys much older than us, and we never saw how predatory they were. I think about a stressful life now, paying bills, being at university, working alongside of university ... but actually, I and a lot of others had it way harder. Don't forget about going through puberty that whole time too. Man, we were brave, fearless, reckless! You might see two young teens on a bus and think, *Aww, how sweet.* When in reality, one's on her way to get drugs to numb her secret childhood trauma and the other is texting a friend telling her to put the razor down for the third time that month. Again, what's even scarier about this is that I'm not even trying to exaggerate. That all really happened. We were kids, but it did not feel like it.

It was this all-girls school that helped with my

social education towards the Muslim community and believers in Islam. As it was an all-female attendance, a lot of parents felt more comfortable sending their Muslim girls to this school. There was an uproar in 2015 (my last year) when my school announced it was going co-ed, which meant it would be taking on boys from 2018 onwards—resulting in the *only* all-girls school in my city transitioning to a traditional mixed school. This had happened with the all-boys school a few years previous.

During my time at senior school, a lot of white and non-religious students would ask the girls with headscarves, "Why do you wear it? Are you allowed to take it off?" I don't think anyone ever asked these things out of disrespect; we were just curious. No one taught us this; we were completely in the dark. It was up to these young girls to teach us white people about their religion, because we wanted to understand it.

Of course there were people who would say offensive things like, "That's so sexist that only girls have to cover themselves", to which the answers were, "No, it's not. It's part of the religion. I want to wear it".

I realised over time that these Muslim girls had battles *every day* educating their fellow students on their beliefs and constantly feeling like they had to justify them. I know we were young, and let down due to being uneducated in such a large percentage of our *own* community—with the only real media we consumed of Islam was terrorist attacks on the news. This left these girls constantly surrounded by their first, second, third, and hundredth experiences of racism and islamophobia at age 12 onwards.

I do feel that by year 11, the last year of senior school, all questions had been answered and a lot of misunderstandings were cleared up, which resulted in a large group of school leavers going out into the world with a clear understanding of the Islam religion and Muslim people. I am naive if I say *everyone*, but I truly believe it was the majority of us. I remember walking home with a girl named Seyema almost every day from school. We would talk about issues of race, and the hardships she suffered. I listened, hearing everything she had to tell me. One day she invited me into her house for a drink, and I accepted. She had a beautiful large house and a garden pond with fish, ducks, and chickens. I was very jealous. I believe I named one of her ducks Jamima Puddle-duck.

When we entered her kitchen, her mother

was washing dishes. She turned round and saw me, stared, and then said something to Seyema in Bengali.

I said, "Hello there", to her mother, to which I received a confused smile. I felt very uncomfortable to be in her home because of this.

Seyema replied to her mother also in Bengali, poured two glasses of juice, and we entered her living room.

"Oh my God, hahah, did you see my mum's face? She was like, 'What? A white person?'" Seyema said, laughing.

"Yeah, I did. Am I OK to be here? Are you going to get in trouble?" I asked, feeling unwelcome.

"No, it's OK. You can stay for a little bit. I do have dinner soon though".

Seyema and I finished our juice and I left, saying a quick, "Goodbye, nice to meet you!" to her mother on my way out. I believe we were about 15 then. Yet I *knew* even at that age why I felt so unwelcome. I wasn't mad; I understood. In fact, I felt so uncomfortable *because* I understood. Why would she want me in her house? I represent the same vile bigots Seyema would tell me about on our walks home. When her mother saw me, I think that's *all* she saw. I was just *so sorry* for that. I never went round Seyema's house again.

Leech and I used to live next to a Muslim family, and we all became very close. It was a single mother, Molly, and her young son, Scott, who was 9 when we lived there. We'd go round her house a lot, and Leech and I even took care of Scott from time to time and helped with school runs. It was because of my time around Muslims I was able cook meals I knew Molly and Scott where allowed to eat too—instead of having to ask, "Is there anything *you don't* eat?" because I already knew the dietary requirements of those who follow Islam.

Once I picked Scott up from school, and he showed me 'tattoos' he had drawn in biro on his arms to copy mine. Although this was the cutest gesture I had ever seen, and I was honoured to be his muse, I had to explain to him that although they did look *super cool on him*—he knew he wasn't supposed to have tattoos when he's older. He did understand this. He was a great kid; I do miss him. (For those of you confused, Muslims do not get tattoos or any other body modifications [piecing's are exempt] because they believe they should die how their God created them. To change the way they look, like with tattoos, is disrespectful.)

Of course I do not speak for the whole of Islam, but I know this is what Molly believed. Islam is such a pure and beautiful religion, and I am an atheist—but hearing those who believe in it and watching them practice it is such an honour. It really makes me realise how little the world knows about it, and this makes me angry. The news and bigots have made their peaceful lives into a destructive nightmare. The reason why I bring up Molly and Scott is because it was thanks to those girls, like Seyema, and my time in senior school that I was able to be educated in their ways. You do not have to participate or believe in order to respect or understand. Muslims are your neighbours. Your colleagues. Your friends. Your business owners. It was Molly's father who actually owned our building.

Ignorance is so dangerous; this world is *not just* yours. Your country is *not just* yours. It is not your way or the wrong way. Do not believe everything the news tells you, they are an institution no different from *Britain's Got Talent*. News only tells us 12 per cent of the world's news, and they pick what will get the most attention and maximum profit. They want to entertain you, make you angry, pander to the bigoted opinions of the many. If you live in the United Kingdom, *please don't shoot the messenger,* but you live in one of the most racist countries on the planet. A planet which is not just yours but everyone's.

I say this with my whole chest: for Scott, educate yourselves. Do better. Please.

12

The University of Maygen X

America's riots sparked by the murder of George Floyd has really caught the attention of everyone. As it should. I have seen so many people post on social media the definition of white privilege. This annoys me, because where were these people when I was sharing posts on Twitter about the injustices? I never got any 'likes' or retweets—I still never stopped. I was trying to spread messages and raise awareness. I believe myself to be consistent in my activism over recent years; however, I feel like a lot of people right now are simply tourists. I talked about the dangers of police brutality against black people in the United States and United Kingdom as much as I could when I saw something on social media that disgusted me. Often met with, "Oh, here she goes again!" but now it's suddenly trendy? I haven't exactly done a lot of footwork in my help to destroy racism, to be honest. I'm hardly the next Malcom X—Maygen X. I just feel like I've done *something*. I mean I'm glad they're somewhat trying to help, but where were you all this time? George Floyd wasn't the first. I knew this. Did they? In a twisted way I wish they didn't, that way their ignorance could be explained. If they did and chose to ignore it until now, shame on them. Activism shouldn't be a trend; I think it's more of a lifestyle and mind-set than something you can just pick up and drop when the mood suits you. I just hope that now because of recent events, it will be a mind-set and fight they never drop again.

You may not believe me, but Eminem's song *White America* is currently playing from my playlist as I write this. (I am a massive Eminem fan.) Interesting that a song written and released in 2002 is still relevant now. Just goes to show in eighteen years fuck all has changed. Life really is shit and then you die. Especially if you're black.

I wonder if we will riot in the United Kingdom due to this. I feel it coming, it somewhat has been mentioned already. I think I remember seeing a post yesterday on social media with hundreds of thousands of retweets saying, "Just wait for one single FU (slang for fuck-up) from British police. We're itching for a riot".

Would I protest and join a riot? I think I would if one broke out in my city. I cannot write everything I have written, believe in everything I believe and not protest. I don't think I could sleep at night being aware of my own cowardice. I think to be part of a riot or protest for such a humanitarian cause would be liberating, fulfilling. Imagine telling that story at parties or to your children? It would go down a treat. I'd definitely be seen as the cool Mum. Being part of a rebellion is without a doubt being a part of something meaningful and bigger than myself—and hopefully it would make a difference. If I survived, that is.

I saw a picture yesterday that actually gave me goose bumps. The image was from the American riots and showcased a row of white women making a human barrier between the riot police and black protestors. These women were dubbed "The Anti Karens". This image perfectly demonstrated how to use white privilege for good. They knew that their whiteness would somewhat keep them safe, so they kept the black protestors safe (well, *safer*). This is also an example of how to truly act in your words and not be an activism tourist. These women were putting themselves in serious danger. So it would seem not all Karens are bad. It sums up the whole ideology around Black Lives Matter; if black lives don't matter, then how can 'all lives matter'? That is an everybody issue. Not black versus white, it is *everybody against racists*. If a riot broke out in the United Kingdom, I hope I would do something like The Anti Karens. I am very short and small, so maybe I could just protect small people or children. That's fine though, I could do that.

My friend and co-worker Asher has been struggling a little bit as of late, due to the isolation. I think everyone has, but some more than others. Since we're now allowed to sit in people's gardens, I invited him to join me, my mum, and Charles in their garden the following day as a way of escapism for him.

In the morning I was woken by Glen our window cleaner washing the kitchen window. I loved Glen; he was only our window cleaner but he's done it for long enough (since I was in senior school) that we've become somewhat friendly. I gave him two bottles of water as it was extremely hot out and we talked about CPVID-19. Glen is a black Christian man and one of the purest souls I have ever had the pleasure of knowing. I thought about the riots in America and if someone was to hurt Glen because of the colour of his skin. I found myself getting protective of him (he's in his late 30s I would presume and very physically fit—I doubt he can't protect himself better than I ever could realistically; but I'd still try). Knowing someone like Glen and then suggesting that because he has increased melanin in his biology he is therefore a worse human being than I am is absolutely ridiculous and idiotic. It is so unbelievably stupid that it borderlines on insanity. And some people have the audacity to call the rioters crazy? They're not crazy at all. They're just *so done* with your bullshit. They're tired. Fuck, I'm tired and it's never even happened to me. Glen's life mattered, I would argue more than others because he's so damn fucking kind, but I don't suppose that's exactly fair either. Glen definitely did matter, though. Everyone in the area knew Glen. He did everyone's windows and spoke to everyone, and I guess you could argue that the whole of Stamshaw to North End was his friend. There's a lot of people that love Glen, and I just hope they'd be there with me protesting if we have to in order to prove just how much it mattered.

I turned up to my parents' house about half an hour before Asher, which gave Charles and me perfect opportunity to talk about *Why I Am no Longer Talking to White People about Race*. He had finished it and even crossed off sections with a pink highlighter and left footnotes. I couldn't believe he took it so seriously. This made me very happy. Then again, was he just trying very hard to prove me wrong? I didn't like the fact that he felt the need to make notes, but I will read the book and find out for myself. I am fair, after all.

"Was there any bits where you thought, 'Ah! I never saw it that way before'?" I asked him.

"Yes. Yes there was", he replied, not really elaborating. "I'll wait for you to read it and you can read my notes and we'll talk more about it then".

He then proceeded to read aloud to me a conversation he had over WhatsApp messenger between himself and one of his friends. He was asked by his friend to go fishing but refused in order to read my book and have it back by Monday—which is exactly what he did. The man gave up a fishing trip for our 'book club'. Wow. Charles read aloud a section where he said to his friend, "Can't go today, mate, I have been assigned homework from the University of Maygen. But Maygen's right in saying that if I'm going to have an opinion, I should know both sides of the debate! So I will indulge her before telling her I'm still right", with a winky face.

I know one might hear this and see a white

male mocking a young activist in her 20s, but from knowing Charles quite well at this point, I see *progress*. I see the humour and understand it is not meant in a disrespectful way towards me (or the cause) but rather a device to lighten the mood on a heavy subject between friends. I also hear the *benignity*. I am not saying that Charles will be one of the people supporting or taking part in the UK riots (if they ever happen), but I think I see his potential to understand his invisible societal pedestal he never noticed before (or chose to not notice). We talked some more about the book after he read me this conversation, and although not *all* of it was agreeable in my humble opinion—he spoke with a different tone than a few days ago. It is with this evidence I use the word progress and am so elated to have been able to potentially teach an old dog new tricks. To be heard, even if it was only slightly. I don't believe Charles could wholeheartedly read a book like that and not come out of it with a new or updated perspective.

Although I still haven't had a chance to read it myself, I just know a book like that has the power to make people understand. I guess the reason why I am not so angry at Charles anymore despite the fact we still don't completely agree on this subject is because he was open minded enough to learn. It's easy to be mad at someone with a 'No, I don't need your input' way of thinking. It's a lot harder to be mad at someone that has a 'Well let me hear your point of view' mind-set. It also could be because I am white and this isn't my prejudice. Yes, I think that's definitely it. I will never understand what it is like to feel this disconnected-personal-hate that is racism. I suppose if a black person was to hear Charles's thoughts, they'd still be very angry. Potentially even more so because his opinions haven't drastically changed despite being addressed with an array of new information. All in all I feel like Charles is on his way to redemption. *It's a start.*

Disclaimer: Having family with problematic or outdated views (to put it nicely) is difficult. You love them, as much as you wish they didn't think the way they did. I understand it must make us look like sympathisers, but when it's family … how can we not love them anyway? I hope you understand this and know that even if these family members were to be disowned, it wouldn't change their opinions. So really, who is it helping? It is more effective if we educate when the moment comes up, argue when it seems necessary and correct them at every moment we can. It is these lasting relationships with such people that can help everyone involved and perhaps change and opinion or two. *It's a start. Perhaps I just tell myself this to excuse my love ones, and by association, myself.*

All I will say is that I will continue to try to change the thoughts of people such as Charles when it comes to matters of race (and other cultural or societal issues); I know it is not going to be a two-day transition and am aware this is a battle that's been fought for a long time; these things are not easily erased. I vow to be as consistent as I can be in my activism and try my upmost to use my whiteness pedestal for good. Unfortunately, for now, that is all I can do.

Mum, Charles, Asher, and I sat in the garden for the whole day. Mum made burgers (and forgot to add the cheese, this obviously ruined dinner). We drank in their tropical Fratton paradise and talked about politics, economics, culture, homelessness, and ghosts. The ghosts were mostly me.

Asher studies architecture at university, so I asked him "Ash, when I become rich and want to build my own house, would you be my architect? I want mate's rates, of course".

Mum asked why I wanted to build my own home and not just buy one already existing, to which I told her that if it's a new house, there will definitely be no ghosts there.

"Have you ever seen a ghost?" Charles asked.

"Well…no. But I do believe in ghosts", I answered. Which is true. I've not had personal experience but I have seen enough YouTube videos.

"So where has this fear come from, then?" Charles followed up.

"Movies", I said.

"Ahh, the movies! Of course", Charles said with a big smile on his face and throwing his hands up in the air.

After a few back-and-forths from the group, which consisted of them mockingly asking me more questions about ghosts, like where I think they live and why they haunt people and so on (which is obvious; they live in the void between life and death and they haunt people because they're tormented spirits), Charles told me something which surprised me.

"You know when I was about your age, maybe a little younger, around 17—I watched *The Exorcist*. It terrified me. It scared me so much that the next day I went down to Portsmouth Market and brought a crucifix. It was a large metal one with a leather chain. The boys on ship (Charles joined the navy at

16) teased me senseless for it. I never took it off. I slept with it on".

"Oh, c'mon, don't take the piss", I said, rolling my eyes.

"No! Seriously. I promise". He did sound serious.

I think the reason I didn't believe him at first is because I can't imagine Charles ever being scared. Of anything. The idea of Charles even jolting at a jump-scare from a scary movie baffles me. I didn't think fear was part of his biology. It's a bit like when you're a kid and you see an adult cry. I remember I saw my mum cry for the first time when her dad died. I must have been around 6. I thought, *Wow, adults cry too?* I just assumed that was something kids grew out of.

Now that I'm 21 years old and wise, I realise all adults cry and for far more serious shit than kids. If you see an adult cry, you know something's fucked up. That shit is heartbreaking. Anyway, I didn't realise Charles ever felt scared. It was weird to imagine. Unnatural. His story made me feel a lot better about my own fear of ghosts, though. If the paranormal can scare the likes of Charles, I guess it was okay for me to be scared too.

"What made you get over it?" I asked him, trying to find a cure to my own fears.

"Pfft, I don't really know. Age? Perspective?" he answered, rubbing his hair.

I suppose if you've lived as long as Charles and gone through a whole lifetime filled with ups and downs, you don't fear things like ghosts anymore. One's fears must become more real, like debts or losing a child. I suppose after a while one's creativity dies too. Your mind stops imagining there's something in the corner of your eye; instead, you just believe it really is just a bit of sleep dust.

We finished up food and drinks so Asher and I said our goodbyes. Asher offered to walk me home. My house was in the opposite direction to his, but he said he didn't mind as it would fill some more time before he went home. I think he just liked being busy. I asked him about his time in the Netherlands. He touched on it when at Mum and Charles's and I kind of already knew some bits. He moved out there to study but it didn't end up going as planned—to say the least. He spoke about how he got himself into debt. He managed to get himself out of it luckily, but at another cost.

"I budgeted myself a limit to spend but it meant I was eating less than five hundred calories a day. I couldn't really afford to eat—I couldn't afford anything. I left weighing 11 stone and came back 8 stone. I think with being a man I felt like I needed to move away and be independent. Independence, though, is a double-edged sword. You can do what you want, but you also have to rely on yourself. You're told, 'Be a man, it's weak to ask for help'. I should've asked for help, but that wouldn't be independence. I was at breaking point. This is why men have such high suicide rates—they feel like they can't ask for help".

Asher was really deep sometimes. We argue a lot at work (because I'm always right), but he was always good at this sort of stuff. I found this really interesting. I had never really asked a guy about his opinions on this or found someone open enough to talk about it.

I asked him, "Did you ever become suicidal?"

"Oh, every day I thought about it", Asher answered, surprisingly perky.

"What made you hold on, to not do it?" I asked, trying to be as sensitive as I could.

"No idea. Determination maybe? Honestly, no idea!" he finished.

This educated me on what it must be like for men. Whilst as a women I am told, "Find a good man to look after you!", men are told "Look after yourself!" This toxic masculinity was killing men. It made me realise that if it wasn't for the patriarchy framing men as the breadwinners, superior, or strong all the time, they could be comfortable enough to admit when they're not doing too well.

It would also allow room for people to feel more empathetic towards men, rather than have a "Be a man!" attitude. The fact that Asher could've died abroad, alone, hungry, and poor through suicide is tragic; just one of those aspects is enough for anyone to reach out. Yet Asher felt like it wasn't justifiable despite the fact he was dealing with all four.

Women must feel like this too, sometimes. I know I have been in some states financially or emotionally and never told anyone; but I would argue that was my choice rather than what was systematically bred into me because of my gender. I always knew I could ask for help and the option was there; I just didn't. Then again, I don't think I've ever been in a situation as bad as Asher's. I feel like if I was Asher in the Netherlands when shit hit the fan Mum or Dad would be on the phone straight away. No hesitation. "Muuuuum, Daaaad, you know I'm your only daughter and you love me? Yeah well, I fucked up". I guess I have this 'thing' to fall back on: "Well I'm only a young girl still; I'll make mistakes".

It seems from Asher's tale men don't seem to really get that. I think from my talk with him I understand more now about men and why their suicide rates are higher than women's. I do think though that if the patriarchy didn't idealise men a certain, toxic way, this issue would be solved. It would seem that feminism and people who campaign for men's suicide prevention are fighting the same battle. Food for thought.

We got to my house and sat on a wall opposite my door, and we spoke about how I was writing my book and Asher's take on religion. I have no idea why Asher starting talking about this, but I would be lying if I said I didn't find it interesting. He explained that if there are gods, he doesn't like the idea of just The One God. Asher prefers the concept of many gods. He spoke about how there is allegedly a bug in Africa that only reproduces by hatching eggs in the eyeballs of young children. I have no idea if this is correct, but I'll just assume he is for the story. He argued that if such a vile thing were to be created by one singular entity, that's really twisted. The thought of one man on a cloud thinking that up and sending it off into the world, for what? A laugh?

I agreed with Asher that it seemed quite totalitarian and barbaric. Asher prefers the idea that if there are multiple gods, then The God of Health could argue with The God of Animals or something and in their fighting make a bug which lays eggs in children's eyeballs—that seems less twisted and more understandable. His idea was that multiple gods can explain the good and bad in life. They can't all agree and they can't make decisions alone. If there is just one big guy (or women or otherwise) one must wonder what his/her/their deal is. I am an atheist, so unfortunately, as much as Asher's concept entertained me, it did nothing for my belief system. It does make me question my belief in ghosts though. Like oh, God's too farfetched, but ghosts are fine? C'mon, Maygen, get a grip.

"I think sometimes I am just kidding myself thinking my book's going to be published", I told Asher.

"Well, do you enjoy it?" he asked me, to which I told him I did. It's true, I really do enjoy writing.

"Then there you go! That's enough. C'mon,

doesn't everyone want to be a writer? It's a pretty sexy job title". Asher always had a way with words.

"Yeah I guess so. It would be cool to be a published author. I do really like the sound of that".

We finished up our conversation on the wall and I went indoors. I saw on Instagram later that evening it was Tom Holland's birthday. Happy birthday, baby!

13

Blood Is Thicker Than Water, but so Is Mucus

Today I was rudely awakened at the ridiculous hour of 10.35am to a delivery consisting of the three dresses I ordered a few weeks back—all exactly the same as the green one I already have (just different colours). Although I wasn't too pleased about being woken, the delivery made the situation a lot better. I was so excited I put the baby pink one on right away. Half asleep, I looked in the mirror at my reflection, and although I resembled a zombie from the neck up, I loved the look of my parachute dress from the neck down. This new arrival demanded I go out into the world to show it off. So I packed my bag and headed out to my aunt Claire's house.

My aunt Claire is a lovely women but not actually my aunt. Claire is my real uncle's partner; they've been together since I was born and she has acted like an aunt towards me my whole life. Claire used to be a nurse and my uncle is a truck driver. In fact, due to my uncle's demanding job, I would argue I am closer to Claire out of the two of them (no offense, D). They live together in a large house, roughly a seven-minute walk from my flat. Despite the short distance, their area is a lot nicer than mine, their street has one of those community spirits where everyone knows everyone and are friendly with one another. One memory I have of their street is Halloweens. Mum would walk me to their road to trick-or-treat. She did this as it was like taking candy from not-so-strangers and a lot safer than the actual strangers around my way. (It avoided the risk of razorblades in apples and such.) They would make us hot drinks and invite us in afterwards. It was a nice time. (Halloween is my favourite holiday.)

I arrived uninvited at Claire's in my new dress, and she welcomed me into her garden (of course it is still forbidden to sit in another household due to the pandemic, but gardens are still fine). She drank tea whilst I drank water and we discussed topical events such as the rioting in America, David Cummings (a politician who recently got into some trouble), the weather, and so on. I liked talking to Claire; we could talk for hours. I always feel a bit less 'heavy' after leaving her house—it's like I've talked all my bullshit out.

She told me her brother had recently discovered the website Ancestry.com and was using his free time during quarantine to do some long-lost-family hunting. She told me how everyone had to log into the account and scan documents they had like birth certificates, marriage or divorce papers, and the likes. It seemed really interesting and a good way to kill time. I wanted to do it. Claire has family in the United Kingdom, United States, and Australia, and from the website they found out her eighth grandparent (or something like that) was the first president/mayor of Australia. That's pretty cool to me. If I found something like that out I'd be walking around like a character from *Game Of Thrones*. "Maygen McDougall, First of Her Name, Great (x8) Grandchild of the Old Leader of this Land, Mother of Luna".

Seriously, I'd have the biggest ego complex. Perhaps it's best if I don't find out my heritage. Although I do believe I am a distant relative (on my mum's side) of the architect Sir Basil Spence, whose work was associated with Coventry Cathedral in England. So I guess there's that?

Claire also told me her late aunt has been found

to have had a secret child in the states, supposedly giving the child up for adoption before returning to the United Kingdom. This has led to Claire and her family trying to find him, who'd be roughly 60 by now. How cool? Imagine being adopted and finding a whole other family decades later. To be honest, I don't know if I'd even bother, they've missed so much is there any real point in connecting the dots now? Claire did argue and say that although her 'technically' cousin would be roughly the same age as her, and he may have children who might also have children, and so on. Also, even at 60, the man might want to know who he actually is. (Remember from my research one's life is less valuable as one ages.) I suppose I would be curious in his shoes. I don't think he'll like what he might find though, since Claire's aunt died very young in a car crash not so many years after his birth and no one knows who his father is. Poor guy.

This conversation made me think about my own situation; how Claire wasn't my blood relative but she's the only aunt I talk to and have. If now, some random women came forward and said, "Hello, Maygen, I am your real aunt", I don't think I'd care. I'd try to get to know her if that's what she wanted, and if she was nice; but she wouldn't compare to Claire. Claire and I have 21 years of history. All me and my 'real' aunt would have is a DNA match. But that's not what humans connect on, is it? Sometimes I see relatives like sisters hang out together but all they do is argue—they normally kiss and make up with the phrase, "But she's my sister". Thing is, if your blood similarity is the only thing keeping you linked, wouldn't it be easier just to detach? I'm not saying disown each other (but that can be an option, I guess) but do you really need to live in each other's pockets just because you're related? I would argue not.

For those of you who use the expression "Blood is thicker than water", allow me to blow your socks off. "The blood of the covenant is thicker than the water of the womb" is the full quote. It means something along the lines of: blood spilt on the battlefield makes for greater ties than that of family. It actually suggests how weak and meaningless family ties are.

My friends will be the uncles and aunties to my children (if I choose to have them). I am an only child and will need to make these choices; but this does not upset me. Friends are the family I can choose. Friends are the family I can bond with over actual values and similarities, rather than just genetics. I prefer this. I know I am biased coming from the world's tiniest family. Honestly, I think I can fit all my immediate family (blood related) on one hand. The rest are the ones I hired as family to do the jobs in the absence of blood. Thank you to Claire, who was also my mum's birthing partner for a majority of my labour as she was on duty in the hospital I was born in (my dad went and played golf instead). Thank you to Rick and Carol for being the other uncle and aunt I also chose, sorry if you felt like you had no say in the matter—you would be correct. Thank you to Charles for being the parent I chose; you've treated me like your own when you didn't really have to. Thank you to Pauline for being the work-mum I didn't ask for but am glad I have. Conversations like this certainly do spark a sense of appreciation in me, I am very lucky to be surrounded by the people I am. I do believe this is because most of them were chosen, though. Not forced.

Disclaimer: I do sometimes look at very close, large families such as Georgia's and observe what that's like. Her family are incredibly close, and all care about each other an awful lot. It would seem sometimes the water of the womb isn't meaningless in every case. All I am suggesting is blood relations aren't everything, and sometimes other types of bonds are just as valuable and meaningful. The point is, be open to both options.

Our discussion turned to the NHS service and the COVID-19 pandemic. As Claire is a retired nurse (RGN), she knew a lot about this sort of thing and how things are run. I asked her lots of questions about her nursing career as it dawned on me although I knew she was a nurse I never actually asked her what it was like. Such an incredible job like that must have a lot to be talked about. I think I was just too young to realise or care until now.

"What was it like? Was there ever times you received a lot of shit from people?" I asked, sat across from her on a wonky, wooden bench in her massive fenced garden.

"Oh, yeah. I had a lot of arguments with people. There were nurses that if they knew they could get away with doing nothing, they would. They'd sneak out for fag breaks all the time. There would be nurses that would be qualified to do things like drug runs, so they'd do that bit then bail out when other work needed to be done. They'd leave the other stuff to the 'unqualified' people (meaning people with no qualification in nursing or pharmaceuticals) like the health-care workers. So the health-care workers would be doing more work for less money and often end up doing things that wasn't necessarily part of their job", Claire explained.

"But I thought you didn't do a job like that unless you want to help people!" I said, getting a little angry.

"Yeah, I know. After a while, people started realising these nurses would only work hard when I was around. On my days off they'd go back to slacking. I said to them [her superiors], I can't work seven days a week to make sure people do their jobs; that's not fair. Sometimes the nurses would stop what they were doing to talk to the doctors, which is fine, but then after the doctors were finished talking to them they'd come up to me and ask, 'So, Claire, what needs to be done?', because even the doctors knew these nurses didn't know what needed to be done and what didn't".

"God, that must have been so annoying! I don't think I could be strong enough to do a hard job like that along with not everyone pulling their weight, I'd go crazy!" I said. Shouting now.

"Yeah, I know, I know. I did enjoy the job. There was good bits. After so many years I did notice a change and just couldn't stand the politics of it all. They'd hire these big finance gurus to run the hospital. Thing is, to them, patients are patients. So in one ward you could have ten patients but they can all look after themselves. In another ward, ten patients that need everything done for them. So logic would say that the first ward doesn't need as much attention as the second. These finance gurus didn't see that, they just saw two wards filled with ten patients each. They didn't see their different needs. They just see money. As time went on we all needed to meet targets such as 97 per cent capacity at all time, reduced A&E waiting times, and so on. If we didn't meet the government's targets, they'd fine the hospital", Claire calmly explained, sipping tea.

"Wait. So the government would take money from a hospital which is funded by the government (and Peoples National Insurance) *if they didn't meet certain statistics? But it's a hospital! Why would you be so robotic!"* I ranted. I was fuming. The logic escaped me. Like, "Oh, your Accident and Emergency times are an hour behind than we would like, so we're going to dock the money you clearly need in order to speed this up". Fucking boomers.

"Yes. So if we didn't meet the numbers the hospital wouldn't be able to buy machinery and things. This is why hospitals are always in debt.

One year, we all worked our asses off. I think we just about managed budget. However, Southampton Hospital was underbudget, so we had to send over any extra money we had to them".

Not once during this conversation did she match my anger. She was cool as a cucumber the entire time.

"So your hard work didn't even pay off?" I screamed, banging on the wonky table.

Sorry I have to leave the story here. My phone is blowing up. One of my female friends is having *another* pregnancy scare. I guess it would seem I am also the family someone else chose, so I may be an aunt to someone myself, soon.

14

Putting My £65 Million Where My Mouth Is

Just as I suspected, the protests in America have spread worldwide, including Denmark, Paris, and the United Kingdom. I'm certain it's happening in other countries as well. This is a really weird time to be living in; it feels like after these protests are over (because like all protests, they come in an end—right?) the world, especially the states, will never be the same again. I saw a post today of a news report from America. It recorded all fifty states (and Washington, DC) are protesting. When was the last time they worked together for anything? The world is not only in a pandemic but a rebellion. Just like the virus had enough of us, we've had enough with oppression. Both have reacted with chaos and destruction—eradicating their hosts.

The weather turned for the worst last night. I

had one of my headaches. Even Asher contacted me and asked, "How's the head?"

I told him it hurt, and he replied, "Ah, damn. I saw a storm predicted on the weather and I just wanted to confirm".

Georgia and I had a nice night despite my headache, though. We sat in my room with the fairy lights on and smoked cigarettes and spoke about our days like usual.

She asked me, "If you could ask one question, any question and you'd get the correct, explained answer, what would you ask?"

This, rendered me silent for a few moments. I was torn. What is the meaning of life? Do aliens exist? Is there a God or multiple gods? Is there a solution to finding world peace?

I answered, "I'd ask for the Jackpot Million lotto numbers for next week—£65 million quid!"

I'm sorry to disappoint. Although, if I was that rich I would spend the rest of my life being a philanthropist and activist (I hope).

Georgia's answer to her own question was, "What happens after we die?"

I thought this was a very good question. It would give one peace of mind. Am I going to hell? Is it reincarnation? Or just a black abyss, like sleep but forever.

In the spirit of Georgia's hypotheticals, I asked her, "If you could ask one question about your future (asking this question would not render it possible to change), what would you ask?"

She thought for a few moments. Whilst she thought, I already knew my answer. "I'd ask the date of my death", I said. I explained that if I knew when it was going to happen, I'd alter my life to fit better around it. If I was told that on 26 November 2025 at 6pm I was going to die, I wouldn't bother finding my dream job. I wouldn't bother with children or love. I'd travel, see the world. I would do lots of different things like skydive and snowboarding. I'd work a job I enjoyed just to pay for stuff, but spend as much time as I could with family and friends. In my last year, I would write a will and set my affairs in order—so it would be a breeze when I was gone.

However, if I was told I was going to die on 15 February 2089 at 3am, I would be a little more relaxed. I would fight for my dream job, I might have lots of children, find love maybe? I would do things that would pay off in the long hall, knowing no one was going to lose me anytime soon.

Georgia actually agreed with me for once and

said she'd also ask that question. This conversation made me evaluate how I *was* living my life. The first or second way? Second, I guess. I definitely wouldn't be going on to do my master's degree if I only had five years left to live. (Although I haven't been accepted yet.) So what was the better way? I guess it would be a happy medium between the two. I want to travel and undertake new experiences, but I don't want to be lonely. I want to live fast—but not really die young. I want that life where I have the white picket fence (an actual fence) and dream job; but don't want to take it all so seriously. I want to be able to tell people cool stories about my life; like the time my friends Milly, Hazel and I started a fight in a vodka bar over a plug-in fan during a heatwave with a group of Navy guys.

This conversation made me think about how I can't really win, its either one extreme or the other. Whether I act one way or another, I might find something wrong with what I'm doing. Sometimes the best plan is to not have one. Technically, that way nothing can go wrong. I guess this is why we never know when it'll all end. Perhaps this is why some, unfortunately, take it into their own hands.

The next morning my boss rang me, which woke me up.

"Are you sleeping?" she asked.

I looked at my phone, and it was 12.23pm. "No", I replied, clearly lying.

"Want me to ring you back later?"

I said no. If I went back to sleep, I might not wake up until after 2pm, which is such a waste of a day.

She'd called to inform me I'll be going back to work on 10 June. She needed staff to go in and prepare the store before opening on the fifteenth.

I gladly accepted, finally knowing I'll have purpose again soon enough. Now I just needed to sort my sleeping pattern out and work out if I can use the bus to get to work. I really didn't want to do the forty-five-minute walk there and back if I could help it. Weird though, now that I know my time in isolation is coming to an end. I have felt so bored and pointless, yet now I know I'm returning back to 'normal', I don't want to leave. Is this how prisoners feel? Institutionalised? I feel like returning to work is going to resemble the scene in *The Shawshank Redemption* where Brooks can't figure out how cars work and is so confused by outside life, he hangs himself. (I cried the first time I watch this scene.) In which case, best start living my life like

I will die on 10 June 2020 at roughly 10am. I will roll a cigarette.

It was now 4 June 2020, and today I took part in the Portsmouth Black Lives Matter protest, which was held at the Portsmouth Guildhall Square. Before I left, I told Georgia I was going, to which she said, "You dick!"

This caused somewhat of a slightly heated discussion in our household.

"Like, I get why they're doing it in America. I really do! But Portsmouth? It is still COVID-19, a crowd is not what we need right now. They keep saying on the news, 'A week of rioting with no new coronavirus cases, wow!' Well just wait another week or so and there will be! Has everyone forgotten it takes two weeks to develop? Mayg, I get it. If it wasn't for the pandemic I'd even go, but what about [inset her ill family members name]?" Georgia explained.

She had a point. It is still lockdown, and the states are doing a lot of protesting and activism on their own. Does Portsmouth really need to do so as well? I explained to her that on the online flyer it specifically says you must come wearing a mask and gloves and still adhere to socially distance rules. I assured her that this is what I was going to do when I went. I explained that although I saw where she was coming from, I *needed* to go. I wouldn't feel right sat at home knowing it was going on just twenty minutes away. I am a firm believer in using your actions (when you can) to join your words. Georgia knows this; she believes the same. She understood why I needed to go.

Just to make sure I wasn't going to be in the doghouse later, I eventually said, "If you really don't want me to go, I won't go. I understand".

"No! I'm not going to tell you what to do, Mayg. That's not what I'm saying. If it bothered me that much, I'd move out for two weeks or something. I still would never tell you what to do. No. I am just making sure you see how stupid this all is. The Summerstown lot might be there—it's Portsmouth! Also what if the police come? If a fight or riot starts, you'll get trampled!"

Although, again, Georgia had valid points, I didn't believe the Portsmouth protest would get violent or rowdy. I thought it would just be what it said on the tin, a peaceful protest standing in solidarity with the George Floyd case (amongst a heartbreakingly load of others) and the #BLM cause. I somewhat sounded naïve, but I just had a little faith that even our town could do some good when it really came down to it.

I promised her I'd be careful and never forget that she has to take care of her sick family member. We found a good middle ground. That's what best friends do. This is what all people should do.

What does one wear to a protest? I had no idea on the etiquette.

This was very important to me. I didn't want to get dressed up or look nice. I felt like that would be disrespectful. Also, if it did break out into a riot, I wanted to be dressed appropriately. I wore Nike trainers, grey jeans, a grey T-shirt, and a navy hooded jacket. Minimalistic, subtle, and I could run or defend myself in it if needed. I also tied my hair into a braid so it was out the way. I put my tobacco, lighter, keys, credit card, earphones, and gloves in the zip-up pockets of my jacket (I didn't think a bag would be necessary) and headed to Guildhall Square. On my way there, I passed a lot of people in the town centre. All of them were either elderly, on mobility scooters, or both. They sat in large groups in circles surrounding coffee huts. Maybe they are a cult? Hilarious because out of everyone, they're the highest risk and a main reason why everything (apparently apart from coffee huts) are closed! They don't even care! Fuming. Seeing so many people in the city centre annoyed me also because they had no excuse to not also take part in the protest that was happening three minutes down the street.

I approached the BLM protest to witness a beautiful sight (kinda). White, black, brown, anything people holding signs (that were double sided as to be read from all angles—very clever) and clapping and cheering at the speakers on the microphone. I stood at the back of the crowd keeping my two-metre distance from anyone I could, keeping my promise to Georgia. The black people that were there made me feel very emotional. In front of where I stood was a tall black man, possibly boy between 17 and 20 years old. Stood with him where two other boys/men. One was mixed-race with blond curly hair (I really liked his hair), and another black male that was definitely a boy and not a man (must have been around 16 years old). They stood there together, very still, silent. Clapping when the crowd did. With this came along another group of similarly aged people of colour, all males. When this group of around five approached the other three, they took turns gently bumping fists and subtly nodding at one another, saying nothing. When they did this, I did not just see friends (they could've been strangers, I honestly don't know) saying hello, I saw a unity. I saw a true connection. It was with every fist bump (they had gloves on) and nod they were saying, "I'm with you". It was quite powerful to watch, especially in the setting where we all were.

I looked at this now rather large group of young men and thought, *God. How could anyone look at you and think you were dangerous?* I started getting upset. I guess they were the reason why I needed to be here. I needed to see them, to hear them and others. Stand with them. I thought about if a riot broke out or if we started getting arrested; I'd run straight for those eight boys. I'd protect them as much as I could. They were boys, they were pure, they were black and proud. It was this moment I felt quite embarrassed being at the protest. I am white. I am not proud to be. The reason why we were all there was all *my* fault.

In front of me were an elderly-ish couple. One was a white male in his sixties (possibly older) and the other was a women, also white and in her sixties (another guess). The man was in an electrical mobility scooter, like the ones in the cult in the town centre I passed on the way there. They stood in the protest cheering with everyone, in embrace the entire time. From what I saw, they were incredibly in love—which is always heart-warming to see. I guess not all boomers are bad after all.

I returned home and texted Georgia as soon as I got in. I told her what the protest was like (slightly implying I was right to have some faith as it didn't get violent) and assured her again I kept my distance from people. I also told her I was safe and untrampled.

She replied, "Glad you enjoyed it and was safe, hahaha", which is about as wholesome as she gets, so I'll take it.

15

Dinosaurs Had it Easy

Upon reflection, the year 2020 so far has been nothing but a shitshow. Iconic basketball player Kobe Bryant and his 13-year-old daughter died in a tragic helicopter crash, which also killed seven other people. In January, there were rumours of a possible World War III thanks to Donald Trump (hardly surprised). Australia was on fire for the whole of February. I think there was a brief time the world thought we were all going to end dinosaur-style due to NASA predicting a meteorite that could possibly hit earth. Coronavirus in March. Now half the globe in rebellion. The global economy is in ruin, people are dying, and no one trusts politicians and the police (less than they did before). As I said, shitshow. What's next?

There are memes at the start of every month expressing comical well-wishes, such as "Congratulations on surviving Jumanji level 3: The

Month of May. Welcome to June, may the odds be forever in your favour".

Space-X sent a rocket into space a few days ago. Georgia and I watched the launch live. Before lift-off, a lot of people were mad at their decision to carry on the launch despite the world's unrest. A lot of people just kept commenting, "This is *not* the year to be doing shit like that". Now I am not a superstitious person (not even a little stitious), but I was in agreement with them. I wouldn't chance it.

Don't worry; the launch was successful and no one was harmed. It seems not everything this year is cursed.

I wonder though: I know all this looks bad on face value—and yes, a lot of tragedy has happened, I'm not arguing that. However, it does make me think, is this the shit year the world needed? The wildfires in Australia made a lot of people realise just how bad climate change has gotten. The Kobe incident made a lot of people grateful for their loved ones; all the money and fame in the world doesn't make you invincible. Accidents happen to us all.

I am trying to think of what hard hitting lesson came out of the Donald Trump fiasco, but, let's be honest. Pretty much 90 per cent of the population really hate that orange cunt. Karma is a sexy bitch, though! The protests and recent events have since brought a lot of shit right to the White House's front door. Protestors rioted outside the White House, forcing all the lights to go dark and Trump to retreat to an underground bunker for protection. Not only that, but secret hacker group Anonymous (if you don't know who they are Google them, they're incredible and worth your time) have leaked information discrediting Trump's reputation (as if they needed to), which included 'proof' that he is a paedophile and showcased naked images of him being spray tanned. Silver linings. As I said before about the #BLM movement, I don't think the world will be the same after all this. Which is a good thing. I hope. Due to all the attention George Floyd's murder has gotten (you might feel better knowing that all four officers responsible have been arrested and charged), it has also heightened the wrongful injustices done to other black people, and other issues with police brutality. It has given people their last straw. Now rioters, protestors, and activists aren't giving institutions and the media *a chance* to cover things up or ignore them. Just like the War Doctor said in *Doctor Who*, "No more".

I hope and believe that although racism will not be totally abolished afterwards (not that I don't wish it was, I'm just thinking realistically), something will be done in regards to police brutality across the world. Subsequently as a by-product of this, prejudice towards people of colour diminishes and people start to see that maybe if *police weren't racist, we'd have far fewer black 'criminals'*. Perhaps the statistics of criminals afterwards would reveal an equal number of black and white perpetrators. Due to this, negative stereotyping around black people starts to unravel. Thus, discrimination decreases—people's mind-sets evolve. Blacks become a bigger active part of society (not because they didn't want to before, but because whites prevented them), supported more financially, socially, and culturally. Being treated with the equality and respect they deserve. The whites are no longer seen as the 'superior' race even inherently, systemic racism starts to die out with older generations and destigmatisation. And so slowly, painfully, like getting blood out of a stone, the world will become a better, less racist place.

> "What if 2020 isn't cancelled? … A year we finally band together, instead of pushing each other further apart. 2020

isn't cancelled, but rather the most important year of them all".
                    —Poet Leslie Dwight

Then again, what the fuck do I know? I'm white. I'm only 21. I've gone to *one* protest and own *one* book about race that I haven't had the chance to read yet and all of a sudden think I'm Martin Luther King Jr.? Laughable, Maygen. Really, I am a bit of a fucking joke. But at the same time, if that was to happen the way I described, it would be another lesson (and somewhat benefit) from this shitshow of a year. I guess that's all I'm really trying to say. I feel 2020 is going to be a turning point of a year. I have faith that although there is a lot of pain right now, not only will the world eventually heal, it will heal improved. I may be wrong. I may have no idea what I am talking about, but if I say that it will be the end of all things good, what would that achieve? Hope can be dangerous; it can also be all some people have. During these times of uncertainty, I choose hope. I come across quite cynical at times, negative and all doom and gloom—but deep down I'm really not. I'm actually quite optimistic. It is this optimism that has prevented me from entering a dark pit of despair. Life *is* unfair, it *is* shit, and then we die; but if all one does is look for bad, I promise you, that is *all* one will find.

Fun fact about me: one of my favourite films is *Girl, Interrupted,* and I often think about a poem one of the main characters, Lisa (played by one of my biggest girl crushes, Angelina Jolie) recites, which I've always thought was quite profound.

> "Razors pain you,
> rivers are damp,
> acid stains you,
> drugs cause cramps,
> guns aren't lawful,
> nooses give,
> gas smells awful,
> *you might as well live!*"

The poem was originally written by Dorothy Parker, and it's called *Resume.*

Take from that what you will.

Georgia came home from spending time at her family, and we fell into our usual routine of discussing our days spent apart. I made her a coffee, and we sat in our living room watching Facebook videos on her phone. She told me about having an argument (technically debate) with her aunt about the existence of white privilege (different aunt from the one she explained it to before). Again, from what she told me it would seem she did another excellent job of explaining the invisible yet completely obvious social structure of whiteness. And again, I was very proud of her. When we're in agreement, we're a force not to be fucked with. We do actually have superhero names given to us by mutual friends, although not very impressive: Boy Tits and Child's Bladder. I'll let you work out who is who and why. We're the dynamic crimefighting duo destroying ignorance at its source since 1999.

Georgia and I sat on the sofa watching videos for the rest of the evening. When it hit around 11pm, we both went to bed. This has also become part of our pattern; neither of us were tired but it's just a way to get these days to end quicker.

On her way to her room, she said, "If you feel like having a fag at any point, come holla at ya' girl". She clearly missed me.

"Yes Ma'am" I replied. I missed her too.

I've been thinking quite deeply about love recently. Because, y'know, my mind never stops. I have been thinking about why it's such a horrible emotion. Its cruel. Its unbalanced. When you love someone, romantically or platonically, you set yourself up for a world of pain. It can make one act in such a drastic way—sometimes completely out of character.

You worry about their safety.

You get jealous they find someone better, or replace you.

They could drop you, rendering you heartbroken.

They could die.

When someone has your heart, that person has power over you. And it goes both ways. I've realised that despite all this, everyone seeks love. Why? Is it the mind-set of, "Better to have loved and lost than to have never loved at all"? I understand pain makes us strong, teaches us things education cannot, but it isn't necessary to survival?

Love is another perfect example of humans evolving too intelligently. We have developed an emotion with no real benefit to us other than it feels good. Cats, for example, do not feel love. They feel security or slight attachment (things humans interpret as love), but not actually love. This makes me sad when I look at Luna, an animal I would kill for, who doesn't even love me back. However, I guess it saves her a world of hurt. What if I rehomed her? At least she'd have the luxury of not giving a shit. I think the reason why as humans we do it to ourselves is because, even for brief moments, it's worth it. The feeling of being in love and being loved in return is so fulfilling—we undertake the risk of getting it all ripped away.

This somewhat reminds me of one of my favourite tales "The Scorpion and the Frog". If you have never heard of this story allow me to tell you. Get cosy and a cup of your favourite hot drink and we'll begin. By the way, this is my own version, so nobody sue me for copyright infringement.

A scorpion needs to get across a lake.

There just so happens to be a frog sat on the same side of the lake, with the scorpion.

The scorpion askes the frog, "Could you let me ride on your back to cross the lake?"

"But what if you sting me?" the frog asked, worried.

"No, I won't", said the scorpion, "That would be silly on my part. You'd die and we'd both drown".

Understanding the scorpion's logic, the frog agrees to travel him across the lake.

Halfway across the lake, the scorpion stings the frog.

With his dying breaths, the frog says to the scorpion, "I don't get it. Why did you do that? Now we're both going to drown".

"Because it is in my nature", replied the scorpion.

I think this story explains some of humans' confusing, illogical behaviour. Sometimes people do things they know are wrong, or just don't make sense, because that is just what we do. It is in our nature. Even if it means we suffer by our own actions. We're self-destructive creators. Emotional psychopaths. We fall in love time and time again, because that is humans' way. I think a lot, sometimes too much. I am the type of person that needs to find reason and purpose and the 'why?' in everything. I am someone who pushes some people away when they get too close. That way if I lost them, it wouldn't hurt. I am someone who finds it difficult to look weak because weakness "Isn't for McDougalls. McDougalls don't get stressed". I am someone who has a nervous laugh, so do not tell me your dog's died in person or I will laugh (happened with an ex-boyfriend once, awful). I am someone who has OCD around the house and finds cleaning fun. I am someone who overthinks if people are 'off' with me; they're probably just quiet or had a bad day.

This, like others traits, is in my nature. Just as everyone, even *you*, have yours.

For every action, there is an equal and opposite reaction. Life is shit and then we die. We create to release extra energy, and destroy what we desire. With chaos comes order. We chose to live fast, or not, and some don't get a choice at all. We know nothing but yet know almost everything.

Because it is in our nature.

I don't know what I am trying to say here. I know I'm not trying to excuse anything, but I think it explains more than you or I realise. I wonder, is this why people say there is a fine line between love and hate?

16

Setting Things not so Straight

When I was around 19, still in my relationship with Leech, I realised I was bisexual. Now, do not think I had 'the wondering eye' necessarily. I was loyal through and through. That does not mean I was blind to my own emotions and feelings. To be honest, I've probably known since senior school. In hindsight it was probably always there.

When I was in Brighton from 2017 to 2019 (gay capital of the United Kingdom), I was surrounded by glorious gayness. I did enjoy my time in Brighton for a lot of reasons, one of them was how freeing the place was. People dressed in extravagant outfits and no one gave a second look. I swear everyone owned a pair of Doc Martens. Even the older generations. There were marches every weekend, trans awareness, climate change activists—you name it, there was a protest/march for it. The people there had tattoos, lots and lots of tattoos. Ah yes, Brighton is gay London by the sea, and it was a very appropriate place for me to live and realise I was, in fact, gay too. However, I couldn't come out. I was with Leech. As much as Leech is very gay-friendly and not homophobic at all, I don't think he would've taken to my coming out very well.

"So, you want to leave me for a girl, is that it?" I can imagine him saying. Or, if he got drunk he might have gotten spiteful and asked, "So what do you think of my friend [inset any female name]? She's hot, isn't she? C'mon, we can talk about this stuff now you're half dyke".

Leech did not say any of these things of course, but you know when you can just *predict* one's reaction to something? I feel like I knew him well enough to know that whatever the case, no matter how not-homophobic he was, it wouldn't have gone well for me. Anyway, I didn't want to tell him. I wanted to leave him and move on with my life. I didn't need him to accept me. I needed him gone.

Months to leading up to Leech and me breaking up, I told Georgia. I think my very words were, "Georg, I erm, think I bat for both sides …"

In return, Georgia gave me the exact reaction I think anyone would ask for. We were sat in a bar one night drinking cocktails and she stood up, with the biggest smile on her face, and threw her arms around. "Oh my God, amazing! Oh my God, yes! This is so cool! Hahaha, I am so happy!"

I eventually ended things with Leech and moved back home to Portsmouth. This is how I ended up back here, and live with Georgia and Luna. See? We're all caught up now. (I finished my last year of university from home.)

I started my current job not long after my move, and where all my co-workers I hadn't met before—I didn't feel the need to come out. Instead, if I had a date with a female or something, I'd slip it into conversation until it clicked. Over a few weeks, if I mentioned a date at work, I'd be met with the question, "Male or female?" I did not mind this. In fact, I quite liked it. I liked that they'd remember to ask. (No one is saying it would make a difference if it was a man or women or otherwise, I think they were just letting me know they acknowledged and respected the fact I was bisexual.)

Next, I told my friend Bonnie. We were very drunk on wine at my flat. Georgia was out this night. I cannot remember how I said it, but I said it.

Bonnie said, "I'm pansexual".

And just like that, two friends who thought they knew everything about one another found out something they didn't. I find it interesting neither of us thought to tell the other sooner. After we both said it, we never mentioned it again. Nothing else needed to be said.

I told another two friends over dinner a month or so after that; these were my two friends from college, Hazel and Milly. Their reaction, I would rate a four out of ten. I won't lie. We were supposed to be travelling to Italy together but due to storms our whole holiday got cancelled. Instead we went out to dinner and shopping to reconcile the holiday we never had. Over desert I said, "OK, so, guys … I was going to tell you in Italy, but since we can't go, this will have to do … I'm bi".

Their reaction was no reaction. They stared at me for a second, both sat opposite to me on the table, then almost in unison said "Oh, OK". In fact, I think one of them said, "Oh, is that it?"

I'm not mad at my friends for this. I think they were just shocked. Also, I think their idea of a 'good reaction' was to not have one. I think their thinking was that it doesn't matter. Which, I agree, one's sexuality shouldn't matter. I think their reaction was to make me feel like it wasn't a big deal and I was still the same Maygen in their eyes. I definitely don't think it was fuelled by judgment or homophobia of any kind. That being said (and I know this sounds picky), but I wish they'd had the same reaction as Georgia. They had no idea that for a few minutes before, during, and after I said 'it', my hands were shaking. I don't know why, they just were. I was nervous. I suppose I can't judge others on their kneejerk reaction to surprises, so that's not entirely fair. You'll be happy to know we're still good friends and since then they have not treated me any different or brought up my bisexuality in conversation.

What I have learned in my year or so of being an out bisexual is that men either love it or hate it. This I find incredibly problematic.

The guys who love it fetishize it: "So explain to me every detail of what it's like to sleep with a women. I'm just curious". Yeah, I'll bet you are, buddy.

"So would you ever like to be part of a threesome?" Yes, but not with you now that you've asked me that.

"Who do you prefer, men or women?" This is the most common one. And I'm sorry, but I do not have an answer for that.

Bisexual means sexually attracted not exclusively to people of one particular gender—that's the gig. If you're bi and you do have an answer for that question, that's fine! But I don't. One of the worst interactions I had was with a male co-worker. I told him a girl was picking me up after my shift, to which he said, "See, I don't think that's fair, to be allowed to have your fingers in all the pies".

Erm, sorry? Fair? Allowed? Oh boy, you sir, are a homophobe. But I was new to the job and so politely replied, "Why not?"

He then expressed his bad luck with dating and all of a sudden it all made sense. My man was just upset he didn't get women and taking his own insecurity out on me. I left him to it.

When I was on my way out and leaving for my date, him walking me to the door, he said, "Don't rape her. You're a wolf in sheep's clothing".

I stopped in my tracks. I turned back around and shouted, "Rape her? Why on earth would you even say that to me! Wolf in sheep's clothing? What do you even mean by that?" I was so baffled, bamboozled. He had rendered me confused. Angry. Taken aback.

I saw the girl I was meeting; she was waiting and I was on a first date—so I just left and tried to recoup myself on the way towards her. I'll never forget that interaction. I don't know what I ever did or said to make him think I was a *predator* (actually I do, nothing … I did nothing).

So with that in mind, let me lay a few things straight (giggity).

1. I do not have twice as much sex as straight or gay people (or any other sexuality). In fact, my experience has left me being rejected or 'ghosted' by more than one gender. I've never had more failure!

2. I do not find *everyone* attractive. If you're a straight female reading this, think about it—are you attracted to *every single male*? Didn't think so. So why am I, a bisexual, attracted to everyone all of a sudden? Yes, I fancy some women, and yes, I fancy some men—but not everything with a pulse!

3. No, I am not a predator. I cannot get *'anyone I want'* as some people have told me. Again, if you're a straight female, can you just walk up to anyone you fancy and get them into bed, no hesitation? No rejection? I'll bet you wish you could (with consent, obviously) but you cant. Guess what? Neither the fuck can I!

I hope this helps you if you ever meet someone

attracted to more than one gender, but I'm sure some of these lessons can be transferred to anyone's sexuality when you really think about it. Look, I don't mind if people ask questions. I get it, you want to learn, understand—you're curious. Nothing wrong with that. The media thinks it's 'with the times', but not as much as it believes. A lot of gayness in things like TV and cinema aren't *that* normalised, they just consist of the gay trope character in TV shows or it's part of the whole LGBTQ+ genre on Netflix. It's either stereotypes or *gay*! Never really normalised. *Especially women*, I feel. You have generally 'normal' gay characters like Capitan Holt in *Brooklyn Nine-Nine* (brilliant TV show 100 per cent recommended) and so on, but I do feel like more needs to be done. My point is I don't mind if people ask me stuff, just ask the *right* stuff. Think before you say it, after all its just attraction—I'm not an alien. I work pretty much the same as anyone else. I also hope it helps if someone comes 'out' to you after you read this. I'm not trying to tell you how to act, or who to be, but please just keep in mind that when I told two of my closest, very tolerant friends of five years, in the year 2020, newly turned 21-year-old adult, my hands were shaking under the table.

It was weird, finally coming clean to myself about my sexuality. It was a long, confusing journey. I felt like part of me took it too late. Like, people 'normally' come out in this generation between ages 13 and 18. I was 19 or 20 years old and only just started to realise. I think a lot of it had to do with the fact I was raised as straight. Straight is 'normal'. However, it's not. There shouldn't be a 'normal' type of sexual orientation. I don't blame my parents for this entirely, they grew up in generations where straight was 'normal'. I hope that if I become a parent, I'll use gender neutral terms when addressing relationships with my children. Rather than saying to my daughter, "When you get your first boyfriend ..." and just assume she'll be straight, I'll say something like, "When you get into your first relationship with someone ..." and so on. I'm no parent or educator, as I have mentioned before, but I like to believe slight changes in language such as that can make a world of difference.

When it clicked I was queer, it was like my brain woke up one day and decided *now! Make her really fancy women the same level as men now! No, not enough gay, we need gayer! Okay, that's better!*

And I, compliant as I could be, went with it. My

first ever date with a women was weird. I feel like I was more awkward than normal. I guess that's to be expected. It was this, that made me personally feel the effects of homophobia. Growing up white and straight, I never really felt prejudice before. In fact, until university in 2017 I didn't really understand the oppression women still suffered. It's been a very awakening three years.

Anyway, this first date with a women was supposed to be in London, but we changed it to Portsmouth in the end and she came to me. That same day (7 June 2019, I believe), two gay women, a couple by the names of Melania Geymonat and her date, Chris, were attacked on a bus in London. The story went viral, as it should. A lot of people's reactions were, "*This* is why there is no such thing as *straight pride*". Which I agree. It's also morbidly ironic, as June is the start of Pride month. Now that really stings.

When I read the story I felt a pit in my stomach. Not like the usual 'oh how awful' empathy. It was, 'fuck, that could've been *me*'. For the first time, I was actually scared to be who I was. I realised that when I 'thought' I was straight, although I hated homophobia and the likes, I never knew how it *actually* felt to be oppressed and fearful. Being a women has its hardships; I was (and still am) scared of rape, for example. But this was new. It was another thing to add to my list of things I shouldn't be scared to be, but I am.

All in all, I have had more negative experiences to my bisexuality than positive. So for anyone who thinks, *Gays are accepted. You can be who you want nowadays. They can even get married in most places now,* and fail to see the discrimination that is in plain sight—shame on you. Don't take it from me, take it from the statistics issued by the Met Police proving that attacks on LGBTQ+ persons have doubled in London since 2014. *Doubled.* It seems the world isn't as progressive as one thought, ay? I saw a statistic on Twitter today about the #Black Lives Matter movement, saying how black trans people's life expectancy is 35. *Thirty-five.*

As I said before, time and time again, about an array of issues (c'mon, say it with me), it's 2020, do better. Refer to my previous chapters on why you need to be educated in certain important issues in order to lose your ignorance. I don't think a lot of people realise that it opinions can save lives.

Disclaimer: I knew about homophobia before I came out, and knew it wasn't easy to be gay in the present day. I went to an all-girls school where LGBTQ+ students would receive all sorts of offensive comments, along with people treating them different and refusing to change around them for PE (physical education). I also do not what people thinking I am gay purely because it is a good 'in'. Sexuality is not a choice, and honestly, after all the bad receptions I've had, I somewhat cannot fathom why someone would choose this life. Choose to possibly be beaten up on a bus, for example.

17

Allonys-y!

And there you have it. The working class are uneducated wasters, the upper class are entitled assholes. We cover up our bodies before having casual sex. Oppressive boys are crushed under increasing suicide rates whilst mean girls are smashed between no consent and hard places. Karens start fighting the anti-Karens. Old judges the new, the young outlive the elderly (*sometimes*). Obsession turns to disgust and love collapses to loathes. Nurses save lives whilst slacking off. White tramples black. Black fights back. We create, destroy and start from scratch. The blood becomes thicker than the water; people do and no not forgive. So, well said before me, you might as well live!

These are the opposites of life, and everything in between. From my humble perspective, anyway.

Something I have noticed, to which I have no answers for; is why it never works both ways.

Tattooed people never judge people without tattoos. Gays never tell straights they're wrong. Men don't get slut-shamed. Why are these scales so unbalanced? Why are the oppressed so empathetic towards oppressors? Is it because we know what it is like to be oppressed, or do we see something the oppressors do not? I notice these opposite sides are never angry at each other in the same way. Whilst one side screams the other is wrong, the other yells back they just want to accepted like everyone else. Perhaps it is because people do not like new things, or change. Maybe it is in the world's nature to have opposites, and thus preventing us from ever reaching complete harmony. Just like Ramsey says in *Game of Thrones*, "If you think this has a happy ending, you haven't been paying attention ..."

I know I've probably contradicted myself during this book. Not in the way where I try and see two sides to arguments. I mean, if I say one thing and then *actually* been unaware I've contradicted myself. I know I've definitely ripped a lot of material from Twitter (to be fair I did say it was academic at times, what did you expect I'm gen-Z). I know I've probably not said something *the right way*, or perhaps just became to obnoxious. I'm sorry if this has happened, please note that if at any point you've felt like this was the case—I didn't mean it that way. Really, I don't. I do not want you to think that I'm here, writing to you, because I am perfect and know everything. I, as a lot of people, maybe even yourself, need to *do better too*. What is vital, is that I, be open to criticism and ready to embrace change, as well as be ready to admit I am wrong sometimes. Take responsibly for ones actions and learn. We are human, we fuck up, we're never all going to agree on everything. This, is in our nature. It is not in our nature however to be perfect, flawless and correct all the time—even when intentions are 'good'. If this is something you've just realised, congratulations. You're on your way to an open mind, clearer heart and improved mindset. Just as everything has opposites, we need to accept failure in order to reach success. Failure is okay, making mistakes is okay—what is not okay is being unwilling to improve when that happens. Everything else, is in between.

Prejudice is humanity's scorpion sting, and perhaps our lake is overflowing with it. Just remember, when the frog and scorpion drowned— who were you to mourn?

I guess this book is just my way of doing something 'bigger than myself'. The idea of people reading this, *you* reading this, and taking even just *one* new perspective away from it; makes me so happy. I guess I just love people, no matter how much we might hate ourselves. Or maybe I just needed to vent. I hope you don't think I'm an egotistical dick now. I suppose even I just want to feel listened too. Please also believe me when I said I tried my very hardest to be all-inclusive and gender neutral when I could, and if at any point I failed, I am sorry. That was never my intention to make someone feel left out or not welcome. In fact, my idea behind this book was so everyone could have something to relate to, something they'd find personal or just plain interesting. My ideal would be that all people, of any background or lifestyle, can read this and find their *something*. I tried to be fair, as un-biased as possible; attempting with my every word to value the beliefs and opinions of the many. I also tried to be funny, I hope at some point during this I made you snort air ever so slightly. I tried to be delicate where I could, and arrestive when I needed to be. I hope you learned something, or felt like you're not alone anymore—maybe even both. Everything mentioned in this book is a true account, recited as accurately as I can remember they occurred. Every conversation was true, every person involved exists (however some names have been altered). This was real life; the good, the bad and the in between.

I guess, along with everything else, that's all I ever really wanted to say.

"I tried to scream,
But my head was underwater.
They called me weak,
Like I'm not just somebody's daughter".
—Billie Eilish, "Everything I Wanted" (2019)

About The Author

Maygen McDougall is a young working-class woman, born and raised in English city of Portsmouth. She was raised by her Mother, in a council flat in Stamshaw. McDougall attended Portsmouth Academy for Girls where she found her love for writing, as well as received her first lessons about issues with gender and race. McDougall concluded her education at the University of Brighton, where she undertook a Bachelor of Arts degree in Media Studies. It was her time in Brighton where McDougall truly found herself, realizing something she hadn't before; as well finding all of the anger she had been missing out on. After her break-up with University boyfriend, McDougall moved back to her hometown where she currently lives with her best-friend Georgia and their cat Luna - this is where McDougall spent her time in writing, amongst the chaos of the Covid-19 pandemic.